THE GOD
WALKING
PROGRAM

to Anthony
May God Bless you
in all that you do.
Keep He With you
Larry Brown Sr.

THE GOD WALKING PROGRAM

Steps Leading Us to the Father's Will

Larry A. Brown Sr.

TATE PUBLISHING & *Enterprises*

Published by Tate Publishing & Enterprises, LLC
127 E. Trade Center Terrace | Mustang, Oklahoma 73064 USA
1.888.361.9473 | www.tatepublishing.com

Tate Publishing is committed to excellence in the publishing industry. The company reflects the philosophy established by the founders, based on Psalm 68:11,
"The Lord gave the word and great was the company of those who published it."

Book design copyright © 2009 by Tate Publishing, LLC. All rights reserved.
Cover design by Jeff Fisher
Interior design by Nathan Harmony

Published in the United States of America

ISBN: 978-1-60799-743-6
Religion: Biblical Studies: General
09.08.24

2 Peter 1:5–9 (NASB)

In your Faith supply Moral excellence, and in your Moral excellence, Knowledge, and in your Knowledge, Self Control, and in your Self Control, Perseverance, and in your Perseverance, Godliness, and in your Godliness, Brotherly Kindness, and in your Brotherly Kindness, Love.

For if these qualities are yours and are increasing, they render you neither useless nor unfruitful in the true knowledge of our Lord Jesus Christ. For he who lacks these qualities are blind or shortsighted, having forgotten his purification from his former sin.

Love is the answer, for every day is his!

Acknowledgments

I would like to give thanks to the following people for their prayers and support, which were of great importance to me.

First of all, I give all the glory to our Lord and Savior, Jesus Christ for his inspiration and help in all things I do.

I would like to thank my wife, Linda, for putting up with the long hours spent on this, and her support in the editing of this book. Thanks for bringing me the large glasses of water, along with all of the encouragement, as I wrote into the wee hours of the morning.

Thanks to all the members of the Bible study for their prayers and support.

A special thanks to Ron and Robyn Hanzel for helping in the research and editing of this book and for their support and encouragement to get it done.

Table of Contents

Introduction

In this book, *The God Walking Program: Steps Leading Us to the Father's Will*, I will show you an incredible expression of love found only in the Bible. We will walk together through the steps needed to understand God's ultimate love, revealing the Father's will for your life.

As we search through the Bible's many hidden mysteries, you will start to understand this incredible expression of love, for the Bible will come alive for you personally.

How much you receive from *The God Walking Program* will be determined by what you believe the Bible to be.

- If you believe the Bible to be a book full of good stories, you will be "entertained"!
- If you believe the Bible to be a good non-fiction novel, you will be "educated!"
- But if you believe the Bible to be the written word of God, then you will be "transformed!"

Let me advise you before you start reading this book: I believe that the Bible is the written word of God, and I study it as so!

This all started one day as the Lord was showing me a marvelous representation of what we have found through our many years together, searching for the Father's will for my life.

It was on a clear and crisp February morning while I was in commune with God. Our conversation started while sitting on the terrace in the back of my house, our thoughts being silent, gazing out at the rays of sunlight creeping over the horizon with a slight breeze hitting my face. It was a beautiful morning.

My eyes were closed as my thoughts reflected on the awesome sight in front of me. I turned to Abba (Father) and told him how I felt. Abba touched my heart and said we should write a book, giving the world a visual view of our relationship.

The sights and sounds of this particular morning were the beginning of a wonderful collaboration with God. Delivering it in written form was both a challenge and a blessing to undertake.

My hope is this: *The God Walking Program: Steps*

Leading Us to the Father's Will; will help God's people grow in a relationship with his Son, Jesus Christ, understanding his powerful word and connecting it with the right of passage we all have on this earth to the Father's will in our lives.

Maybe someday someone who is searching for truth will read *The God Walking Program* and experience the growing phenomenon between their created bodies and the awesomeness of God as they journey together on their way home.

Let's pray.

> *Father God,*
>   *May this book be your will and your thoughts, guiding our minds and hearts to a relationship with you. May your Holy Spirit in truth and understanding be the guiding light to your will in these writings, to whoever shall pickup this book and read it.*

For the reader:

> *Father God, I pray that the Holy Spirit touches you and leads you into a relationship with our Lord and Savior, Jesus Christ, finding the Father's will for your life. I ask this in the name of Jesus Christ, my Savior.*

The Bible

Let's talk for a minute. We need to get something straight from the beginning before we start studying my word.

You must believe that the Bible is a book written by the inspiration of my Holy Spirit and believe it with an unwavering heart. If you think that man alone wrote the Bible about me, not with me, then the idea that you can have a relationship with me is unrealistic.

You might as well put *The God Walking Program* down and pick up a comic book or a book with fictional content where its leading character wins at every turn, controlling the outcome.

As the reader, you get nothing, no interaction with the author, little, if any, involvement in real life defeats or victories. You get nothing to grasp on to or hope for, only a false sense of security that your own strength will empower you. In reality, you're left with emptiness.

My word was written by my Spirit to help you understand my heart. With every stroke of pen, I will show you how my word was written with you personally in mind.

This is my invitation to you. If you accept, let's begin!
It will always be your choice; I will never interfere.
I love you unconditionally!

—Jesus

In the beginning was the Word, and the Word was with GOD, and the Word was GOD

John 1:1

The Bible is an amazing book narrated by a God of love; it discloses its mysteries to all who are willing to partake.
The Bible is...

- ...a book of truths that have withstood the intense scrutiny of the historic and scientific community's findings throughout the ages.
- ...a book with magnificent stories that date back six thousand years and reveals minute details of God's love for us.
- ...a book written in a flowing, graceful manner with writers of various social levels and professions; it is woven together by the powerful Holy Spirit

with the common thread of God's love like an expensive floor covering laid out for the world to examine and admire or to trample on and discard.

- … a book that gives you the confidence of knowing you're not alone.
- … a book that guides you through all life's experiences with the expectation of victory, knowing the Creator loves you and wants to have a relationship with you.

When exploring the Bible, we all come to realize the mystical awe of God. A relationship between a created being and his creator is uncovered within its pages, revealing a true and unconditional love that extends straight from the Creator's heart to the created extension of himself.

Studying the Bible with an inquisitive mind and open heart will help you immensely in your journey through this cruel world. So let's read and study it together, allowing our Lord and Savior to guide us, knowing that his intention is to lead us toward the Father's will in our lives.

There are books out there that are very good in helping you understand the ailing parts of your life. There are also many books out there that will give you a glimpse of satisfaction in their attempts to solve your problems. But you will always crash in your spiritual walk unless the solutions are tied to this great book, the Bible.

When a doctor looks at your physical problem, he utilizes the vast years of studying and learning from the library of medical books at his command. While studying your condition, he or she can draw on this wealth of knowledge within these books, uncovering the reason for your ailment and giving you his or her recommendation in solving this problem. Doctors are a blessing from God; and God uses their solutions to heal this worldly body.

The Bible has the same wealth of knowledge within its pages for spiritual matters and should be treated with the same respect and professionalism as a doctor, healing the spiritual and physical bodies in all of us.

The Holy Spirit

This great book was written by the inspiration of the Holy Spirit; and when the Holy Spirit stirs in us, we can be assured that his written word is alive and well, helping us move toward the Father's Will.

Sometimes he's our instructor, teaching us the spiritual aspects of a situation, giving us the confidence to move closer to the Father.

Sometimes he's our guide, directing our thoughts into a communication with the Father, guiding us into a loving relationship with the Son.

Sometimes he's our protector, correcting us with a soft, but firm, nudge, avoiding a particular situation in our lives, delivering us from certain destruction or developing us in wonderful victories.

The Holy Spirit is our guide; he directs us to a relationship with the Son, allowing us the opportunity to achieve the Father's will in our lives.

In every case, we will grow and develop into the Father's will, while helping others in love.

Larry A. Brown Sr.

The words of the Bible are alive and moving; all this activity is to help us grow in our relationship with Jesus Christ.

The Bottom Line

By accepting the call of the Father, creating a relationship with his Son, and walking in that relationship, you will receive the fruits of the Spirit, living a peaceful, fruitful, and collaborating existence while moving into the Father's will for your life.

This is how it happens:

The Bible is the inspired word of God.

The *Holy Spirit* is his helper, guiding us toward the Bible into a relationship with his Son.

His Son is our instructor, giving us an understanding of these inspired words from God while moving us toward the Father's will in our lives.

The Father empowers us to do his will.

This is the Triune Spirit of God: God the Father, God the Son, and God the Holy Spirit.

> Peace I leave with you; my peace I give to you: not as the world gives you. Do not let your hearts be troubled, nor let it be fearful.
>
> John 14:27

Section 1: Let's Start from the Beginning

I was reading the Bible as a young Christian, and I came across a statement that really puzzled me. The passage that I am referring to was John 1:29.

"Behold the lamb of GOD who takes away the sins of the world."

It made me ask: *If God took away the sins of the world, then why was there sin?*

By asking this one question, I was driven into a life-long study in the wonderful, stimulating word of God! It all started when I asked for God's intervention, praying,

"Father God, thou are my God, and thou will help me understand thy greatness of thy power."

Then I heard a voice in my spirit saying, "Stop! What are you doing?" *What was that?* I thought. The voice continued and said, "I am."

My response, looking back, showed me that I was a great scholar of the Bible. "I am what?"

"My son, you're giving me a headache. I already know who I am. I even know who you are. The real question is do you know who you are or why I created you?"

That really startled me, and my head dropped. I was ashamed of my prayer life. This was the only way I knew how to communicate with God. I was following the group, and it wasn't working for me.

I decided right then and there that I was going to get right with God and converse with him, asking the how and why questions.

"Lord, you get headaches?"

"No! I do not get headaches, this was a metaphor, such as the parables my Son used before the new covenant began. I love all my children and listen intensely to their prayers.

"What saddens me is this: My children are trying to communicate with me using their own mythology. Praying to a God in a language he doesn't understand in an arena where he's not.

"They need to know how to find me, understanding what I am saying and allow me to participate. My people need to know the Bible speaks to their hearts and how it applies to them.

"They can only achieve this in a relationship with my

Larry A. Brown Sr.

Son. He will guide them to an understanding of my will. The closer they get to my Word, the closer they get to me."

Let me show you how this works—the closer we get to the word, the closer we get to God. Here is an Old Testament example where, by asking the how and why questions, your eyes will be opened to a biblical reality.

> And Melchizedek king of Salem brought out bread and wine; now he was a priest of God most high. He blessed him (Abraham) and said; blessed be Abram of GOD most high, Processor of heaven and earth and blessed be GOD most high, who has delivered your enemies into your hand. He gave him a tenth of all.
>
> Genesis 14:18–20

"Lord," I asked, "why did you place these verses into the text, when it had no basis to the story?"

"This is what I mean by asking the why question. You have noticed the verse before and after concern Abraham's victory and his interaction with the king of Sodom. Let's look at the text before and after."

> Then after his (Abram's) return from the defeat of the Chedorlaomer and the kings who were with them, the king of Sodom went out to meet him at the valley of Shaveh (that is, the king's valley)…The king of Sodom said to Abram, "Give the people to me and take the goods for you." Abram said to the king of Sodom, "I have sworn to the LORD GOD most high,

processor of the heaven and earth that I will not take a thread or sandal thong or anything that is yours, for fear you would say I have made Abram rich."

Genesis 14:17, 21–22

"You saw how I inserted verses 18, 19, and 20 and had the presence of mind to ask why. It was very important that you saw this and communicated this to me. Let me show you how important it was for you to ask!"

For this Melchizedek, king of Salem, priest of the most high GOD, who met Abraham as he was returning from the slaughter of the kings and blessed him, to whom Abraham apportioned a tenth of all the spoils, and was first of all, by the translation of his name, king of righteousness, and then king of Salem, which is king of peace. *Without father, without mother, without genealogy, having neither beginning of days nor end of life, but made like the Son of GOD,* he remains a priest perpetually. Now observe how great this man was to whom Abraham, the patriarch, gave a tenth from the choice spoils.

Hebrews 7:1–4

But the one whose genealogy is not traced from them collected a tenth from Abraham and blessed the one who had the promises. But without any dispute the lesser is blessed by the greater.

Hebrews 7:6–7

"Now let me ask you a question? Who was Melchizedek?"
"He was our Lord, your Son," I replied.

Larry A. Brown Sr.

"The Holy Spirit has revealed this to you."

I fell down to one knee and started to pray: "Open my heart, Lord, and reveal all things to me by your Holy Spirit in your written word."

"By studying the Bible in relationship with my Son and asking the important questions of how and why, my word will come alive in you."

> Jerusalem, Jerusalem, who kills the Prophets and stones those who are sent to her; how often I wanted to gather your children together, the way a hen gathers her chicks under her wings, *and you were unwilling.*
>
> Matthew 23:37–38

Then the Lord says something that saddens my heart. I cannot imagine how he feels when his people keep turning on him.

"They need to believe in the omnipotence (power) and omnipresence (always present) of a loving God."

"This must have made you feel terrible! I know that I have rejected you many times. Please forgive me."

"This has always broken my heart. I am a forgiving God. All my children need to do is turn around (repent) and come back to me. We would have kept moving toward their destiny in this world."

Wow! I thought.

"Let's look at the Hebrew meaning of Jerusalem. I think you will enjoy this."

The Hebrew meaning for Jerusalem: Jeru-salem; place of peace; the city of he who is perfect.

And he carried me away in the spirit to a great and high mountain, and showed me the holy city, Jerusalem, coming down out of heaven from GOD, having the glory of GOD. *Her* brilliance was like a very costly stone, as a stone of crystal-clear jasper.

Revelation 21:10–11

I saw no temple in it, for the Lord God the Almighty and the Lamb is its temple.

Revelation 21:22

"Wow! Not only was Melchizedek our Lord your son, but Salem is the representation of your holy city and bride."

"See what you would have missed by not asking why? In studying the word, you will have to see and understand the mysteries to understand the truth."

"Let man regard us in this manner, as servants of Christ and stewards of the mysteries of God.

1 Corinthians 4:1

Jesus answered them, "to you it has been granted to know the mysteries of the *kingdom of heaven*, but to them it has not been granted."

Matthew 13:11

And He said, to you it has been granted to know the mysteries of the *Kingdom of* GOD, but to the rest it is in parables, so that seeing they may not see, and hearing they may not understand.

Luke 8:10

Larry A. Brown Sr.

"I noticed that there were mysteries in the kingdom of heaven and in the kingdom of God. Are these two different places?"

"Yes, and I will show you later in this book how important this really is. The Holy Spirit was sent into your heart by my Father to teach you the mysteries of his Word. In our relationship, I will help you understand his teaching, guiding you into his will. Now you can see why it is so important to have a relationship with me."

> He who believes in the Son has eternal life; but he who does not obey the Son *will not see life*, but the wrath of God abides on him.
>
> John 3:36

"You need me to be your tutor, protector, and instructor, guiding you into my Father's will. This is very important, so listen! You can accept the call of the Father and *choose not to have a relationship with me*, trying to understand the mysteries of the Holy Spirit and the Father's will for your life, or you can accept the call of the Father, *choosing to have a relationship with me*; I will protect you, interpret the Bible for you, and guide you into the Father's will. The choice is yours. I will not interfere! There is so much to learn! A lifetime to do it in!"

Section 2: Ask, and I Will Answer

"I am, He is, and you are. Let's just start with that."

- I am God
- He is my Son
- You are my chosen

When you accept my Son, my Spirit comes into you, and you become *saved [from Him]*.

Romans 8:9

These are the steps we need to take as we move into his will:

- (From him)—accepting Jesus as your savior
- (Through him)—a relationship with Jesus Christ
- (God's will)—being used by God for his purpose

When you start communicating with my Son you have a *relationship* [through Him].

Romans 8:10

When your relationship with my Son grows, we will come and abide in you and you become God's will [to Him].

Romans 8:11, John 14:23

For *from Him* and *through Him* and *to Him* are all things. To Him be the glory forever. Amen.

Romans 11:36

"Lord how do I get through these steps?"

There was silence, no response. An emptiness enters my body. I can feel my heart pounding. I thought my conversation with God was over! Was it because of my stupidity or my stubbornness? What was wrong?

"My word. Let me show you."

A big grin came upon my face. Was it because the emptiness had gone away, or was it the nervousness about what was about to happen?

"I have no aspirin up here, so just listen."

I felt a chuckle in my heart and smiled.

"When I wrote my word (the Bible), I interjected interac-

Larry A. Brown Sr.

tive thoughts so my people can have a relationship with me. With this communication, I can show them my thoughts, guide them in the yearning of their hearts, and bless them as a father should; but sadly, most refuse my help."

"Not me!" I sighed.

Let's continue in the beginning. Genesis 1.1: "In the beginning, God created the heavens and the earth."

That made sense. No questions yet, but then came verse two:

"The earth was formless and void, darkness was over the surface of the deep, and the spirit of GOD was moving over the surface of the waters."

I had to ask myself why. Why would God make the earth in this condition (void, darkness)?

"Good question. Go to Revelation 12:7–9."

> There was a war in heaven, Michael and his angels waging war with the dragon. The dragon and his angel's waged war, and they were not strong enough, and there was no longer a place found in heaven for them. The great dragon was thrown down, the serpent of old who is called the devil and Satan, who deceives the whole world; *he was thrown down to the earth*, and his angels were thrown down with him.
>
> Revelation 12:7

> The seventy returned with joy, saying, Lord (Jesus), even the demons are subject to us in your name. And he said to them, "I saw Satan fall like lighting from heaven."
>
> Luke 10:17–18 (NKJV)

"You were there when all this was happening?"

"I was!"

This started the questioning that God had expected by choosing me.

Please, don't worry. I will not ask all of them, just the ones Abba deems necessary for this book. Here are a few:

- Was earth created for the fallen angels?
- Could the earth have been created way before Adam?
- Is the heaven stated in Genesis 1 the same heaven the war was in?

It says heavens (plural) in Genesis Why? Come. Let's find out.

> He established the earth upon its foundations, so that it would not totter forever and forever. You covered it with the deep as a garment; the waters were standing above the mountain.
>
> Psalm 104:5–6

> For when they maintain this it escapes their notice that by the word of GOD the heavens existed long ago and the earth was formed out of water and by water.
>
> 2 Peter 3:5

"Lord, how could this be? You created the heaven and earth at the same time in Genesis 1:1?"

"I want you to look at how I spelled heaven in this text."

I looked and noticed that it said heavens; it was written in a plural tense. "I see what you are saying. What does that mean?"

> I know a man in Christ who fourteen years ago—whether in the body I do not know, or whether out of the body, I do not know, God knows—such a one was caught up to the third heaven.
>
> 2 Corinthians 12:2 (NKJV)

Then he said something that made me pause.

"Time is a modem for travel, like sound and light; it is the essence of all things. The heavens—or sometimes called expansions above the earth—are not where you can find me. It is a dimension in time, put in place until I return with my Son, and we will live with the chosen ones."

> Then I saw a new heaven and a new earth; for the first heaven and the first earth passed away and there was no longer any sea. And I saw the holy city, the New Jerusalem, coming down out of the heaven from GOD, made ready as a bride for her husband. And I heard a loud voice from the throne, saying, Behold the tabernacle of GOD is among man, and HE will dwell among them, and they shall be his people, and GOD himself will be among them.
>
> Revelation 21:1-3

"Wow! That was amazing! I can't wait to be with you in person."

"I will greet you with a smile. As you can see, I created the Earth and covered it with the deep as a garment, and it existed long ago. That was written a thousand years before my Son entered into the world. I created the Earth for Satan and his angels, and I sent them there because of their sin, as seen in Revelation 12:7. This was done before I created man."

"Why does this matter?"

"This will help you understand the relationship with evil versus the relationship with love. We will cover this later."

"God, take full control of this, and we'll go along for the ride; God what about Adam and Eve?"

"Then GOD said, 'Let us make man in our image, according to our likeness'" (Genesis 1:26) (NKJV).

"What? It says let us? In our...? Who are you talking to, us and our? God, what is this all about 'in our image'?"

> And let them have dominion over the fish of the sea, over the birds of the air and over the cattle, over all the earth, and over every creeping thing that creeps on the earth.
>
> Genesis 1:26 (NKJV)

> God created man in *HIS own image*; in the image of God He created *him* male and female He created them. GOD *blessed them* and God said *to them* "BE fruitful and multiply, fill the earth and subdue it; have dominion over the fish of the sea; over the birds of the sky and over every living thing that moves on the earth."
>
> Genesis 1:27–28 (NKJV)

"Wow! What was that? He created man in *his* own image, male and female, and blessed them? There was only one man created, and you keep saying them as if there were two. How can this be?"

> This is the book of the generations of Adam. In the day when God *created man, in the likeness of God made he him;* Male and female created he them; *and blessed them and called their name Adam* in the day they were created.
>
> Genesis 5:1–2 (KJV)

"I am still a little uneasy with this. Can you explain more?"

"Maybe this will help you. Go to John 4:24."

> *God is Spirit* and those who worship must worship Him in spirit and truth.
>
> John 4:24 (NKJV)

> Behold My (Jesus) Hands and My feet, that it is I Myself; handle Me and see, for a spirit does not have flesh and bones as you see that I have.
>
> Luke 24:39 (NKJV)

> So God created man *in HIS own Image; in the image of God* He created *him* male and female He created them.
>
> Genesis 1:27 (NKJV)

"So God is a spirit. That means that man was in spirit form because he was created in his image? Right? Okay, then why male and female?"

And the Lord God formed *man* of the dust of the ground, and breathed into his nostrils the breath of life; and *man* became a living being.

Genesis 2:7 (NKJV)

So God created man in His own Image; in the image of God He created *him* male and female He created them.

Genesis 1:27 (NKJV)

And the lord God commanded *the man*, saying, "Of every tree of the garden you may freely eat but of the tree of the knowledge of good and evil you shall not eat, for in that day that you eat of it you shall surely die."

Genesis 2:16–17 (NKJV)

"So what you're saying is that Adam had a male and female in him?"

"Yes."

"So how did Eve come into being?"

Then the Lord God said it is not good that man should be alone; I will make him a help mate for him.

Genesis 2:18 (KJV)

So GOD caused a deep sleep to fall upon *Adam*, and he slept; He took one of the ribs (curved side) and closed up the flesh instead thereof. And the rib which the Lord God had taken from man, made he a women, and he *brought her unto man*.

Genesis 2:21–22 (KJV)

"Why didn't you have to breathe into the women's nostrils as you did with the man, bringing him to life in Genesis 2:7?"

"The woman I took out of the man was already alive in him. This happened when I breathed life into his nostrils."

"So she was already there, right?"

"Yes, she was. This is also why I created animals first as a helper for Adam instead of the woman."

> "Out of the ground the lord God formed every beast of the field and every fowl of the air and brought them to Adam to see what he would call them"
>
> Genesis 2:19 (KJV)

"So, Lord, am I correct in saying that when Adam and Eve were separated in Genesis 2:22 they became two separate beings?"

"Right! This is the reason why women have only the X chromosome in them, while the man has X and Y chromosomes."

"So when they come back together as one flesh, what happens?"

> "Therefore shall *a man* leave *his father and mother* and shall cleave unto his wife and *they shall become one flesh*."
>
> Genesis 2:24 (KJV)

"Wow! Man was created in your image, the image of God, with both male and female characteristics. You separated these characteristics into two separate beings. When these two separate beings come together *in one flesh*, they are in fact, at that time, the image of you, the image of God. Right?"

"Right!"

"This is so cool."

"You're starting to understand. This is why it is so important to be married to an equally yoked person."

> Marriage is to be held in honor among all, and the marriage bed is to be undefiled; for fornicators and adulterers God will judge.
>
> Hebrews 13:4

> Do not be bound together with unbelievers, for what partnership has righteousness and lawlessness, or what fellowship has light with darkness?
>
> 2 Corinthians 6:14

"When the man and the woman become one flesh, they become a reunion of my creation as I originally made it. Adam's statement in Genesis 3 is a beautiful rendition of this. I wrote it down to show you that I am in all things, literally, if you will allow me."

"Are you saying that woman can only have a relationship with you in marriage?"

"No! Anyone can have a relationship with me, single or married, but remember woman was created as a helper for man."

> And Adam said, "This is now bone of my bones, and flesh of my flesh; she shall be called Woman, because

Larry A. Brown Sr.

she was taken out of Man. Therefore a man shall leave his father and his mother and shall cleave unto his wife; and they shall become one flesh."

Genesis 2:23–24 (KJV)

"Woman, when she is united with man in marriage as the helper, completes the reconstruction of the man as he was originally created."

"Woman is the ultimate helper for man; they bring the essence of spiritual oneness with you, right?"

"Right. Understanding of this spiritual oneness by both the man and the woman is a powerful ingredient in our walk together. It allows me to have their full attention as I teach them the steps to the Father's will for their lives."

"Is this why you have chosen to use a female trait when you talk about wisdom in your word?"

> How blessed is the man who finds wisdom and the man who gains understanding. For *her* profit is better than the profit of silver and *her* gain better than fine gold. *She* is more precious than jewels; and nothing you desire compares to *her*.

Proverbs 3:13–15

"Lord, then why do some men treat women as second-class citizens?"

"They are very foolish and do not understand my word. My covenant is with man, and he is accountable to me; the woman must respect that as the helper. But man must also understand this: women have my characteristics in them, such as wisdom. There is a oneness with me in togetherness."

> Or do you not know that the one who joins himself to a prostitute is one body with her? For he says, "The two shall become one flesh." But the one who joins himself to the Lord is one spirit with Him.
>
> 1 Corinthian 6:16–17

"One of the greatest gifts given to man was the helper, the woman you created from the curved side of man. This gives man an incredible boost in achieving the will of the Father, becoming one in the Lord. This is so powerful when you really understand it. Remember, unequally yoked marriages bring about a cancerous growth that needs to be healed before this oneness can be achieved. On the other hand, equally yoked marriages can start growing right from the beginning. The blood is always the answer!"

"Now we have established that Adam and Eve were in a perfect environment and relationship. So what happened?"

"Remember Revelation 12:7, the fall of Satan to the earth?"

"Yes."

"Now go to Genesis 2:16."

> The Lord God commanded the man saying, "Of every tree of the garden you may eat freely but from the tree of the knowledge of good and evil *you shall not eat, for in that day you will surely die.*
>
> Genesis 2:16 (NKJV)

"Now go to Genesis 3:4–6."

Larry A. Brown Sr.

The serpent…

"Is the serpent mentioned here Satan from Revelation 12:7–9?"

"Yes it is."

"So Satan was already there as you told us."

"Yes, he was with all the fallen angels!"

> The serpent said to the woman, "You will not surely die! For God knows that in the day you eat from it your eyes will be opened and you will be like God, knowing good and evil." So when the woman saw that the tree was good for food, that it was pleasant to the eyes, and a tree desirable to make one wise, she took from its fruit and ate.
>
> Genesis 3:4–6 (NKJV)

"So why didn't anything happen to her when she ate the fruit?"

"The covenant was with Adam (Genesis 2:16), not with Eve, and she gave also to her husband and he ate."

> And the eyes of both of them were opened, and they knew they were naked; and they sewed fig leaves together and made themselves aprons.
>
> Genesis 3:7 (NKJV)

As you can see, when Adam ate the fruit, the covenant was broken and both their eyes were opened to Satan's sin. Once Adam disobeyed me, the covenant of the garden was over."

"So this is why they were driven out of the Garden of Eden?"

"No."

> Then the Lord God said "Behold, the man has become like one of us, to know good and evil; and now, lest he put out his hand and take also from the tree of life, and eat and live forever. Therefore the Lord God sent him out from the Garden of Eden, to till the ground from which he was taken.
>
> Genesis 3:22–23 (NKJV)

"So this was why man was driven out, because you loved him so much? You knew that he could not survive with the knowledge of good and evil and live forever?"

"Yes."

"What happened to Satan in this?"

> I will put enmity between *you* and the woman, and between *your seed and her seed*. He shall bruise you on your head, and you shall bruise his heel.
>
> Genesis 3:15 (NKJV)

"Who are you speaking about when you say 'you' in this passage?"

"Read the verse before."

"Okay."

> The Lord God said to *the serpent* (Satan), "Because you have done this, you are cursed more than all the cattle, and more than every beast of the field; on your

Larry A. Brown Sr.

belly you shall go, and you shall eat dust all the days of your life."

Genesis 3:14 (NKJV)

"In Genesis 3:15, the 'you' is referring to Satan, right?"

"Right."

"The text is talking about Satan's seed and woman's seed. Are you talking about children?"

"Yes."

"So Satan can have children?"

"The word seed has the same meaning for Satan as it does for Eve."

"Wow!

"Lord, I want to apologize; not for all the things I have done badly in my life, because you already died for them, but for *not understanding* or, more importantly, *understanding* that you have always been here and still ignoring you. Forgive me and grant me sensitive ears to hear, powerful eyes to see, and the strength to overcome. I do not want to overlook your presence ever again!"

"When you accepted me as your Savior, you already received the things you're asking for. Why do you doubt the things I have said in my word (the Bible)?"

As for me (John the Baptist), I baptize you with water for repentance, but He (Jesus) who is coming after me is mightier than I, and I am not even fit to remove his sandals; He (Jesus) will baptize you with the Holy Spirit and fire.

Matthew 3:11

"I have already done this! Move in my strength, for my grace is with you."

"You have taken care of me. You were there…

- …in my early days of trouble. I did not know you and didn't care to.
- …when I was sent to Vietnam. You protected me from harm and other untold things.
- …through all my studies, giving me inspiration and guidance when I never asked you for it.
- …when my children were born, Christina and Christopher, and when they died.
- …when I cursed you and decided that you were the blame for my loss.

You were there…

- …when Heather and Larry were born; this was a great blessing to me, but I put my job first.
- …when I met my wife, Linda—a wonderful gift from you, a soul mate. I didn't deserve this.
- …when I finally gave up and accepted you, asking for a relationship.
- …when I felt your loving touch on my heart.

"Lord, now I know all that I received. It was the love you demonstrated for me on the cross, transferring it to me at the resurrection and growing in me during our relationship together. We are walking together into the Father's will for me, moving toward the final destination: Him. Thanks for being there."

"Always!"

Larry A. Brown Sr.

For He Himself has said, "I *will never leave you, nor will I ever forsake you.*"

Hebrews 13:5

Please understand this (Follow this closely, and you will understand.):

"When Adam ate the fruit, he opened the door to the Earth where I sent Satan and his angels (demons, nephilim, giants). Most people believe that when Adam ate the fruit, sin entered the world. It did; it entered my world, where I placed Adam! Sin was already on the Earth because of Satan's fall. When I created the Garden of Eden, I blocked Satan's sin from the minds and eyes of my created one, creating *my world or kingdom* on Earth! When Adam made his choice to eat the fruit, they were sent into Satan's sin, allowing Satan's sin to be understood by my created beings. I then blocked Satan's sin from reentering my world by placing cherubim at the entrance, closing the door to *my* world on Earth.

"By making a choice to be obedient to My call and accepting My Son as your personal Savior, My Spirit is sent into your heart, placing you in the saving grace of myself.

My new world let me explain:

- My Son removed the cherubim's, which I placed at the entrance to my world (the garden); stopping all from entering.
- He then positioned himself at that same entrance, allowing anyone who accepts him as their savior to enter into Himself.

Delivering all who accept out of Satan's sin, into (my saving grace) my new world. Jesus.

Now that you have entered My new world, you have the *opportunity* for a personal relationship in his sinless self. As you move in *this relationship with Jesus. He will* nurture you through the word (Bible) into My will for your life!

Let's put it all together

When you accept My Son as your personal savior, you receive my saving grace, which is a free gift (God the Holy Spirit). This grants you access to eternal life.

Now that you have my saving grace living within you, what happens? You have two choices;

Stay where you are; not growing or moving, storing no treasures in heaven...or you can move into a relationship with the second part of the triune spirit (God the Son).

My Son will move you into the third part of the triune spirit Me (God the Father) while blessing you with the fruit of His spirit storing all your treasure in heaven. (John 14:23-Romans 8:11)

Section 3: God is the Reason for Victory

You must understand Revelation 12:7 to follow the next passages. When I sent Satan to the earth, a third of the angels (now demons) in heaven fell with him. Keep this in mind as we move along in our conversation."

> Now the man had relations with his wife Eve, and she conceived and gave birth to Cain, and she said, "I have gotten a manchild with the help of the Lord." Again she gave birth, to his brother Abel.
>
> Genesis 4:1–2

> And Cain talked with Abel his brother: and it came
> to pass, when they were in the field, that Cain rose
> up against Abel his brother and slew him.
>
> Genesis 4:8 (KJV)

"Why did Cain kill Abel?"

"Jealous of my gratitude toward Abel; it was a matter of *choice*. I instructed him to try harder and with more thought, and he chose this instead."

> But for Cain and for his offering he had no regard.
> So Cain became very angry and his countenance fell.
> Then the Lord said to Cain, "Why are you angry?
> And why has your countenance fallen? If you do
> well, will not your countenance be lifted up? And if
> you do not do well, sin is crouching at the door; and
> its desire is for you, but you must master it."
>
> Genesis 4:5–7

"This is a problem today. My word teaches people what to do in any situation. If you do not understand this, just ask for wisdom, and my Father will give it to you freely."

> If any of you lacks wisdom, let him ask of God, who
> gives to all generously and without reproach, and it
> will be given to him.
>
> James 1:5 (NKJV)

"A lot of times when they ask, they choose not to follow! This happened with my people in the Old Covenant, and it is happening now. I loved Cain, but I would not inter-

Larry A. Brown Sr.

fere with *his decisions,* and you can see what happened. Take a look in Genesis 4:9."

> Then the Lord said to Cain, "Where is Abel your brother?" And he said, "I do not know. Am I my brother's keeper?"
>
> Genesis 4:9 (NKJV)

"I would think you would have already known what happened to Abel, so why did you ask him?"

"As I did with his father, Adam, I gave them both the opportunity to trust in me. They decided not to. Remember Genesis 3:9 when I called out for Adam, asking him where he was? What was his reply?"

> So he [Adam] said, "I heard your voice in the garden, and I was afraid because I was naked; so I hid myself." I asked him, "Who told you that you were naked?" The man said, "The woman whom you gave to be with me, she gave me from the tree, and I ate."
>
> Genesis 3:10–13 (NKJV)

"Can you see I was giving both of them the opportunity to repent and continue in a true relationship with me? But *they chose* not to!"

"Yes. Sadly, I can."

"My people need to know that I love them and died for them so they can be truthful with me! I will get them through anything, as I wrote in Galatians 6:1, Matthew 7:7–8, and Romans 8:1."

Brethren, even if anyone is caught in any trespass, you who are spiritual, restore such a one in a spirit of gentleness; each one looking to yourself, so that you will not be tempted.

Galatians 6:1

"As you can see, I commanded the Galatians, the ones who loved me, to bring their people out of their sinful ways."

Ask, and it will be given to you; seek, and you will find; knock, and it will be opened to you for everyone who asks receives, and he who seeks finds, and to him who knocks it will be opened.

Matthew 7:7–8

Therefore there is now no condemnation for those who are in Christ Jesus.

Romans 8:1

"By having a relationship with me, you can count on my leading you in the right direction to the Father's will.

"Following this guidance, you will be protected and blessed with the fruits of the Spirit.

"For when I look at myself, I see God!"

"So what you're saying is that we can trust you?"

"Absolutely and without fear!"

I am the way, the truth, and the life! No one comes to the Father except through me.

John 14:6

Larry A. Brown Sr.

Section 4: The Whole Thing is Falling Apart!

"Now that we know what happened to Adam and Eve, what happened to Cain?"

"Now you [Cain] are cursed from the earth which has opened its mouth to receive your brother's blood from your hand. When you till the ground, it shall no longer yield its strength to you; a fugitive and a vagabond you shall be on the earth. And Cain said to the Lord, " my punishment is greater than I can bear!" "Surely you have driven me this day from the face of the ground; *I shall be hidden from your face*, I shall be a fugitive and a vagabond on the earth and it will happen that anyone who *finds me will kill me*."

Genesis 4:11–12, 14 (NKJV)

"What did that mean, 'they will kill me'? Who are 'they' if Adam, Eve, and Cain were the only people on the earth at that time? Are the evolutionists right?"

"No, they are not right! Let me explain. Remember reading Revelation 12 from earlier?"

"It was about the fallen angels you sent to Earth that you created for them after the war in heaven a long time ago. Right?"

"Right."

Let the love of the brethren continue. Do not neglect to show hospitality to strangers, *for by this some have entertained angels without knowing it.*

Hebrews 13:1–2

For our struggle is not against flesh and blood, but against the rulers, against the powers, against the world's forces of the darkness, against the spiritual forces of wickedness in the heavenly places.

Ephesians 6:12

Let no one in any way deceive you, for it will not come unless the apostasy comes first, and the man of lawlessness is revealed, son of destruction, who opposes and exalts himself above every so-called god or object of worship, so that he takes his seat in the temple of God, displaying himself as being God.

2 Thessalonians 2:3–4

Larry A. Brown Sr.

"Let me understand this. Both angels of God and demons of Satan can show themselves in the form of humans?"

"Yes. Now you will understand what happened next and what happened to cause the flood."

"The flood? Are we going there now?"

"Not yet, but this is the beginning of the end. Let's go back to Cain. After I drove Cain out from his people, he married."

> Then Cain went out from the presence of the Lord and dwelt in the land of Nod, east of Eden.
>
> Genesis 4:16 (NKJV)

"When Adam was created, there were at least two places. There was Eden—that is where you placed the garden—and there was another place called Nod, right?"

"Right."

"So Cain married somebody from Nod. He couldn't associate with anyone from Adam and Eve because he had been banished, right?"

"Right."

"So there must have been other people here before Adam or at the same time as Adam, right?"

"No. Adam was the first man, but there were the fallen angels from Revelation 12. As we learned, they can be in the form of humans."

> And I will put enmity between *you* (Satan) and the woman, and between *your seed and her seed*; he shall bruise your head, and you shall bruise his heel.
>
> Genesis 3:15–16 (NKJV)

"So Cain married a fallen angel?"

"The Spirit has reveled this to you."

"It is all about the bloodline!"

"It will always be about the blood. This created two blood-lines: one from Adam called the sons of God and one from Cain called the sons of man. The sons of God were: Adam, Seth, Enosh, Kenan, Mahalalel, Jared, Enoch, Methuselah, Lamech, and Noah. The sons of man were: Cain, Enoch, Irad, Mehuahel, Methushael, Lamech, Jabel, Jubel, and Tubel-cain. I will now explain what happened at the flood."

> Now it came to pass, when men began to multiply on the face of the land, and daughters were born to them, that *the sons of God* saw that *the daughters of men, that they* were beautiful; and they took wives for themselves of all whom they chose. There were Nephilim [fallen angels, giants, demons] on the earth in those days, *and also afterward*, when the sons of God came in to the daughters of men, and they bore children to them.
>
> Genesis 6:1–2, 4 (NKJV)

> God looked on the earth, and indeed it was corrupt; for *all flesh had corrupted their way upon the earth.* And God said to Noah, "The end of all flesh has come before me; for the earth is filled with violence *through them*; and behold, I will *destroy them* with the earth."
>
> Genesis 6:12 (NKJV)

"The flood was because the sons of God had children with the fallen angels and they became flesh, therefore leaving no righteous in the world, right?"

Larry A. Brown Sr.

"Right."

"Does the statement in verse 4—"the *Nephilim (fallen angels, giants, demons)* were on the earth in those days, *and also afterward*"—show us that they did not die in the flood, only the cross-blooded people died? Noah was the last of the sons of God right?"

"Right. 'The cross-blooded people' an interesting choice of words. But you are right."

"Why would they die?"

"They (the Nephilim or demons) were in the same situation when I sent them to the earth in Revelation 12:10, after the war in heaven. Now that I flooded the earth, it would be no problem for the Nephilim (giants, demons) to adapt to it as they did before!" (Revelation 12:10; Genesis 1:1, 9). Can you name whom I chose to save from the flood?"

"Okay. There was Noah and his wife; they had three sons: Shem, Ham, and Japheth. Each son had a wife. There were eight in all. Eight people and Satan and his nephilim sounds like trouble to me!"

"It is all about the blood, and it always will be."

Section 5: The Road to the Law

"Lord, I thought your chosen people had learned from their father's misfortunes. But I guess not, looking at the next few chapters. You always want to help us, don't you?"

"Yes, I am always here; it is very easy to have a relationship with me by reading my word (Bible) and communicating with me."

> Come to Me all who are weary and heavy-laden, and
> I will give you rest. Take my yoke upon you and learn
> from Me, for I am gentle and humble in heart, and

you will find rest for your souls. For My yoke is easy
and My burden is light.

Matthew 11:28–30

In the beginning was the Word, and the Word was
with God, and the Word was God. He was in the
beginning with God. All things came into being
through Him, and apart from Him nothing came
into being that has come into being.

John 1:1–3

"Lord, the 'he' that was with God in the beginning, that
was you?"

"Yes, it was!"

"So you are saying all things came into being through
you?"

"Right again."

"Wow! Now we have a friend who is all!"

"And for you personally!"

Then the LORD said to Noah, "Enter the ark, you and
all your household, for you alone I have seen to be
righteous before ME in this time."

Genesis 7:1

"Lord, you said to Noah, 'you are the only one righteous,'
but not any of his family. Was the reason because the covenant was with man?"

"In this case, he was the only one and the last of the
first."

"I thought that Noah brought two of each animal species onto the ark?"

"Obviously, you saw the next verse. The real problem is you *thought*! That's a very dangerous problem with my people these days; they think they have the answers. However, they're finding these answers from others at work, on the playground, from people whom I don't even know; they even find answers from sources I find repugnant. You *thought* wrong! But I love you anyway, and now you know the unclean animals were two pairs of each kind.

"My clean ones were seven pairs, male and female, of each kind (Genesis 7:2). The only answers you will find to be true are found in the Bible (my word)."

"Lord, I must have hit a sore spot. I am sorry!"

"Not at all; I'm used to it!"

My heart saddened quickly, knowing what I put my Lord through! He still loves me, even when I'm stupid. You're not stupid, my son, just uninformed!"

"Go to Revelation 3:14."

> Unto the angel of the church in Laodicea write:
> These things saith the Amen, the faithful and true
> witness, the Beginning of the creation of God
>
> Revelation 3:14 (KJV)

"Wow! We'd better listen to this with open ears and great thought!"

"May I continue?"

"Okay."

> …I know your deeds, that you are neither cold nor
> hot; *I wish that you were cold or hot.* So because you
> are lukewarm; neither hot or cold, *I will I spit you out*
> *of my mouth.*
>
> Revelation 3:15–16

"What does that mean?"

"This happens when you're in a relationship with me;
when you are cold, I *can* work with you. When you are
hot, I *am* working with you. Both stimulate your growth
in me. But when you are lukewarm, not growing in me
and not moving toward the Father's will, we have no use
for you. And I will start the relationship over.

"Remember! I will never leave you or forsake you. We
will just start our relationship over again if you choose to.
The choice is yours to continue with me or just stay out.
I will be excited or saddened by your decision, depending
on which you choose."

> My little children, of whom I travail in birth again
> until Christ is formed in you…
>
> Galatians 4:19 (KJV)

> But speaking the truth in love, we are to grow up in
> all aspects into him who is the head, even Christ.
>
> Ephesians 4:15

> As newborn babies, desire the sincere milk of the
> word, that ye may grow thereby, if so be ye have
> tasted that the Lord is gracious.
>
> 1 Peter 2:2–3 (KJV)

Larry A. Brown Sr.

But grow in the grace and the knowledge of our LORD and Savior Jesus Christ. To Him be the glory, both now and to the day of eternity. Amen.

2 Peter 3:18

"As you can see, I place a lot of emphasis on having a relationship with me, a relationship that has to be wanted and started by the choice you make. We might have to start over and over again, but I will always be there with you. Let's grow together into the Father's will for you."

"Okay."

"Let's continue with Noah. Noah had three sons: Ham, Shem, and Japheth."

Then Noah began farming and planted a vineyard. He drank from the wine and became drunk, and uncovered himself inside his tent.

Genesis 9:20–21

Wine is a mocker, strong drink is raging, and whosoever is deceived thereby is not wise.

Proverbs 20:1(KJV)

Ham, the father of Canaan, saw the nakedness of his father, and told his brothers outside. But Shem and Japheth took a garment and laid it upon both their shoulders and walked backward and covered the nakedness of their father; and their faces were turned away, so that they did not see their father's nakedness. When Noah awoke from his wine, he knew what his youngest son had done to him. So he said, "Cursed be Canaan (Ham was the father of the Canaan); a servant of servants He shall be to his brothers." He also said, "Blessed be the LORD, the GOD of Shem; and let Canaan be his servant. May GOD enlarge Japheth, and let him dwell in the tents of Shem; and let Canaan be his servant."

Genesis 9:22

"Wow! What a mess Ham put his descendants in by dishonoring his father."

Cursed is he who dishonors his father or mother. And all the people shall say, "Amen."

Deuteronomy 27:16

"Now we have a problem. The blessing has gone to Shem and the curse has gone to Ham."

"The flesh has started all over again with their evil heart. But remember what it's all about."

"The blood, right?"

"Right!"

The Illustration

"My son, do you remember the time when we were all sitting in the front yard? Your sister was there with us. You had just turned thirteen."

"No, I don't recall."

"It was the time when your big toe was cut badly."

"Yes, I remember it now. Why?"

"Let's show the reader what happened and how I was there for you. Tell them the story."

My sister and I were at home one morning; it was a beautiful morning. The sky was blue and the day was hot. We knew our friends would be at the river swimming, so we asked to go. Mom was gone, so we asked our stepfather.

"Did I tell you that my sister and I were the biggest twins ever born in New York, and—"
  "I already know that. Continue!"

My stepfather told us he had to leave; he then proceeded to handcuff us to each other and had us sit in the middle of the front yard. I was wearing shorts, a tee-shirt, and tennis shoes. I don't remember what my sister was wearing.

"Didn't you yell at your father?"
  "He wasn't my father! He was my stepfather."
  "You yelled at him when you asked him if you could go swimming with your friends!"
  "No! You were there; you should know!"
  "Yes, I was. Continue."

It was a really hot day. We were fighting off mosquitoes with no prevail. They were biting us everywhere. We sat in the middle of the yard for a long time. I couldn't take it any longer. So I said to my sister, "Let's get out of here!" So we left. The plan was to go swimming and get back before they got home. It was a two-mile walk to the spot where all of our friends would be swimming.
  There we were, walking down the road

handcuffed, both feeling as if we were escaped convicts, ducking as cars passed; I guess we were just amusing ourselves, trying to cover up our embarrassment. I don't remember how we got the handcuffs off. Maybe our friends helped us. They were all aware of our home life.

"Tell them about the toe!"

I was running up the hillside when I smashed my big toe on a rock. The blood began pouring out. Dragging my foot, I struggled to continue. Finally reaching the ridge, I pulled myself up, thoroughly exhausted. My toe was throbbing. Blood was gushing out all over the place. My sister quickly wrapped my foot up with my shirt and helped me over to where we left our shoes. They were gone! Apparently, my stepfather took them because they were on the porch when we got home. As we walked the two miles back to the house, we anticipated the trouble we were in. *It isn't going to be a good night,* I thought. As we got closer to the house, I could see the porch light was on. Clinging to my sister's arm, we started toward the house. The pain was throbbing, reaching up to my knee now, and the limp was worsening. When we were close enough to the house, my sister called out for help; no answer. We walked up to the porch to open the door, but it was locked. The blood was seeping through my shirt now. Not knowing what to do, we assumed our original position on the lawn. The pain was creeping through my body, and I was getting tired. It wasn't long after we sat down that my grandmother pulled into the driveway. Noticing there was something wrong; she

Larry A. Brown Sr.

got out of the car and ran over to me. Undoing the makeshift bandage my sister had managed to create for me, she examined the problem and saw what she had to deal with. They helped me to the porch. Pulling out her keys and unlocking the door, she went in. As they sat me on the chair, she said, "We'll fix you right up." When she came back outside, she was holding a bottle in her hand. As she came closer, I could see it was a bottle of *iodine*!

"The pain moving up my left side was bad already, but *iodine!* I was sure you were taking me home, Lord, after she poured the first *gallon* on my foot!

"My grandmother—'Grams' as we all called her—was the same person you were trying to get me to go to church with, Lord."

"She's not the one."

Puzzled by his response, I continued.

I didn't know what she was doing; I was concentrating on how to get to the iodine bottle and throw it across the street. My toe was wrapped with Popsicle sticks and bandages as Grams tries to comfort me with her smile. My sister helps as they lead me down the hallway to the bedroom. Grams gives me a pill as she helps me onto the bed.

As I started to drift off, I could hear Grams voice saying, "Tomorrow I will come by and take you to the doctor's. He'll fix you up right." Whatever she gave me, it worked, and I went to sleep.

When I got up the next morning, I expected the onslaught of yelling; there was none. Going to the front door, I opened it and walked out. No one asked, and no one came after me. I never went back to that house again.

"Lord, why did you let this happen? You were there, weren't you?"

"I was there; I always am."

"Then why?"

"My son, this is a reality you need to understand. I was teaching you to take more responsibility with your own children and take more control of their lives."

"What do you mean? My children are Christians, and they love you."

"Yes, I know that, but they will fail unless you have the handcuffs ready and waiting for them."

"My children will never have to go through what I went through!"

Laughter! I heard laughter. Where was it coming from?

"It's not me!"

"Lord, is that you?"

"I was not the one talking to you; it was Satan. This is one of the ways he tricks my people (as he did in the garden with Eve), trying to pull you away from me. His tactic is to make you think I am the one causing all your difficulties, trying to discourage you from seeking a relationship with me. Your children, as well as your grandchildren, are safe and walking with me. I was there protecting you. It wasn't a coincidence that your grandmother drove up."

"I know that Abba loves me!"

"I always will!"

"When having a relationship with me, you will learn my voice and not be tricked by Satan's schemes."

> My sheep hear My voice, and I know them, and they follow Me; and I give unto them eternal life, and they shall never perish; neither shall any man pluck them out of My hand.
>
> John 10:27–28 (KJV)

"This is how *the accuser* works. That is what Satan means in the Greek: wimpy and powerless. He comes imitating me."

> Be of sober spirit, be on the alert. *Your adversary, the devil,* prowls around like a roaring lion, seeking someone to devour.
>
> 1 Peter 5:8

"Notice the words?"

"Yes, I noticed that Peter said 'adversary.' Isn't that the Hebrew (Old Testament) way of saying Satan's name? Why didn't Peter describe Satan as the 'accuser' (New Testament) in this text?"

"Peter was talking to the Jewish people, reminding them that Satan was trying to imitate me. Satan was trying to persuade *my chosen ones* that he was to be feared."

"He has no authority to do this!"

"My Father's roar is a powerful and consuming roar, a warning sound of the destruction about to happen to the people who have not accepted the Father's saving grace: me!"

"So Satan's roar is trying to stop the called ones from receiving the blessing of salvation, right?"

"Right!"

"It also means that Satan has no roar in the salvation grace of God. *Satan cannot hurt us.*"

"Right! As long as you are in a relationship with me, Satan has no power at all."

> Therefore there is now no condemnation for those who are in Christ Jesus.
>
> Romans 8:1

"I am always there watching out for you. Just listen to my voice, and I will guide you back or stop you from going. It is in the depth of our relationship that determines how fast you respond.

"The accuser is always trying to fill you up with yourself, the same self you're denying in me."

"We all have difficulties in our lives, some being extremely difficult. When we accepted Jesus Christ as our personal savior, we can now win this battle once and for all. Satan *cannot* hurt us, because the Spirit of our living God is in us."

"Right!"

> And do not be conformed to this world, but be transformed by the renewing of your mind, so that you may prove what *the will of God is*, that which is good and acceptable and perfect.
>
> Romans 12:2

Larry A. Brown Sr.

For all who are being *led by the Spirit of God*, these are sons of God.

Romans 8:14

Remember who the sons of God were.

It's about the blood!

> For *you have not received a spirit of slavery* leading to fear again, but you have received a spirit of adoption as sons by which we cry out Abba, Father. The Spirit himself testifies with our spirits that we are *children of God!*
>
> Romans 8:15–16

"Do not get caught in the realm of Satan's schemes. Get into a relationship with me. I will guide you, and together we will grow into the Father's will."

"Shouldn't we get back to Noah? I feel a little embarrassed right now!"

"Don't be embarrassed, for all my children have to be aware of *Satan's schemes*; they need to be taught how to respond when it happens. As our relationship grows, this understanding becomes apparent, and the outcome is already decided.

"Amen! It is a relief to have someone guiding us through these ordeals."

"I am always there for you!"

> Know therefore today, and take it to your heart, *that the Lord, He is God* in heaven above and on earth below; there is no other!
>
> Deuteronomy 4:39

"Amen!"

"Let's go back to Noah. Now Shem received the blessing from God."

> So he said, "Cursed is Canaan [Ham's descendants]; a servant of servants he shall be to his brothers." He also said, "Blessed be the LORD, the GOD of Shem; and let Canaan be his servants."
>
> Genesis 9:25–26

"As you can see, there is a problem arising between brothers."

> And a Canaanite woman from that region came out and began to cry out, saying, "Have mercy on me, LORD, Son of David; my daughter is cruelly demon-possessed." But He answered and said [to his disciples], "I was sent only to the lost sheep of the house of Israel." And He answered and said, "It is not good to take the children's bread and feed it to the dogs." But she said, "Yes LORD; but even the dogs feed on the crumbs which fall from the master's table." Then Jesus said to her, "O woman, your faith is great; it shall be done for you as you wish." And her daughter was healed at once.
>
> Matthew 15:22, 24, 26–28

> And Andrew, and Phillip, and Bartholomew, and Matthew, and Thomas, and James the son of Alphaeus, and Thaddaeus, and *Simon the Canaanite.*
>
> Mark 3:18 (KJV)

"Lord, what's happening here? You placed a Canaanite on your staff."

"Remember, it is all about the blood. The bloodline comes from Shem, and the blessing to the world will come from his bloodline. I am starting to graft the rest of the world to me."

"It is all about the blood."

"Abram was my chosen one from the beginning. Why don't you summarize what we have just gone through? There are very few characters to deal with; it should be very easy to follow."

"Okay. In the beginning we saw God creating Adam. God saw that Adam needed a helper and the helper eventually became Eve. Satan was the adversary and was trying to persuade Eve to break the rules. Just like today, the accuser is trying to make us look like hypocrites to this world. If Adam had the understanding of the power of the Holy Spirit, we wouldn't be in the saving grace of God right now. He didn't, and fell to the schemes of the adversary. This opened our minds to the understanding and the realization of pride. Pride is the killer of what our Father wants to achieve through us. Satan needs this thought pattern (pride) to survive in the schemes he inflicts on this world.

"We then saw God's love for Adam protecting him from the tree of life by blocking his access to reach out and devour it. Knowing that with this knowledge of sin he would be in agony, God shortened his walk through the world. Now that they are out of the garden, we see what happens when pride enters.

"The first murder in the short history of the world enters, as well as the punishment of being banished from the face of God. This action created a mixture of nephilim and flesh, creating the sons of man. The two bloodlines clash and the great flood occurs, thus the end. But not quite. God saw one man's righteousness and saves him and his family. That man was Noah. God then chose Shem from the offspring of Noah. Noah put a curse on Ham, driving his offspring to servant status. This leads us to Abram."

I want to emphasize that this is a basic overview on what happened during this period of time.

The Bible has so much to offer that our book could not possibly cover the wealth of knowledge contained within its pages; only by studying its vastness can you find the truth.

"Lord, can you give us some examples of these?"

> Then Enoch walked with God three hundred years after he became the father of Methuselah, and he had other sons and daughters. So all the days of Enoch were three hundred sixty-five years. Enoch walked with God; and *he was not, for God took him.*
>
> Genesis 5:22–24

"You had a personal and physical relationship with Enoch while he was on earth?"

"Yes."

"What was the reason you took Enoch? Was it to show us that you could?"

"Not just for that reason. This was 1151 years before Noah was born and was the period of time when the sons of God started their interactions with the sons of man. I chose to take Enoch out because of his relationship with me, just like I am going to do in the last days when the antichrist shows up. I will choose to take out my church in the same manner as I did with Enoch, taking the people who have a relationship with me. Enoch was ready when I came; so should you be!

"Here is another example that you may like."

> Now the man called his wife's name Eve, because she was the mother of all the living. The LORD GOD made garments of *(animal) skin* for Adam and his wife, and clothed them.
>
> Genesis 3:20–21

"Does that mean that the animal skin that God covered them in was to cover their spirit bodies because they were still in spirit form at that time?"

> It is sown a natural body; it is raised a spiritual body. There is a natural body; there is also a spiritual body.
>
> 1 Corinthians 15:44 (KJV)

"The Holy Spirit has revealed this to you."

"That makes a lot of sense now! When God created man, he created him in his image. God is a spirit, as we found out in John 4:24, right?"

"Right."

> GOD *is a spirit* and they who worship Him must worship Him in spirit and in truth.
>
> John 4:24 (KJV)

"This is why the scientists have found that humans have the same DNA as a certain species of monkey, excluding the twenty-fourth strand.

"When I 'clothed' man, I used animal skins. I used this skin to cover the man's and the woman's spiritual bodies, protecting them from the harsh environment they were being sent into. These skins contain the DNA of that animal. This is what the scientists are seeing today."

"This would answer a lot of questions, wouldn't it?"

"Remember, I'm in control and always will be. You can always trust me."

Larry A. Brown Sr.

Section 6: Chosen of God

"Let's start this section with a list of people. Can you name the people I have chosen to work with so far?"

"Okay. Here's the list."

- Adam
- Enoch
- Noah
- Shem

"These have all been my choice and from one bloodline."

"So we can come to a conclusion: the blood is of value to you."

"The blood is always the answer."

> No longer do I call you slaves, for a slave does not know what his master is doing; but I have called you friends, for all things that I have heard from My Father I have made known to you. You did not choose Me, but I chose you and appointed you that you would go and bear fruit, and that your fruit would remain…If the world hates you, you know that it has hated me before it hated you. If you were of the world, the world would love its own; *but because you are not of the world*, but I chose you out of the world, because of this the world hates you.
>
> John 15:15–16, 18–19

"Does this mean you have already chosen the ones you want to use from the beginning?"

> Blessed be the God and Father of our Lord Jesus Christ, who hath blessed us with every spiritual blessing in the heavenly places in Christ, *according as He hath chosen us in him before the foundation of the world*, that we should be holy and without blame before Him *in love*.
>
> Ephesians 1:3–4 (KJV)

"Yes. Unfortunately, some refuse."

> Therefore I say to you, any sin and blasphemy shall be forgiven, but blasphemy against the Spirit shall not be forgiven. Whoever speaks a word against the

Larry A. Brown Sr.

Son of Man, it shall be forgiven him; *but whoever speaks against the Holy Spirit, it shall not be forgiven him, either in this age or the age to come.*

Matthew 12:31–32

"What does this mean?"

"This is a very important question to understand, so listen closely. When my Son died on the cross, all sin was taken away from his chosen ones—the ones who accept my call to have my son as their personal Savior. Some people hear this call clearly and refuse to accept my Son as their Savior. This is what is called 'Blasphemy of the Holy Spirit' (refusing to be obedient to my call). My Son has already died for their sins. I will not let him go through that again."

"Why would anyone refuse the call from you?"

"Sadly, they do!"

He that overcometh, the same shall be clothed in white raiment; and I will *not blot out* his name out of the book of life, But I will confess his name before My Father and before His angels.

Revelation 3:5 (KJV)

All who dwell on the earth will worship him [Satan], everyone whose name *has not been written* from the foundation of the world in the book of life of the lamb who has been slain.

Revelation 13:8

And someone came to Him and said, "Teacher, what good thing shall I do that I may obtain eternal life?" Jesus said to him, "If you wish to be complete, go and sell your possessions and give to the poor, and *you will have treasure in heaven*; and come, follow Me." But when the young man heard this statement, *he went away grieving*; for he was one who owned much property.

Matthew 19:16, 21–22

"Wow! He could have been one of the apostles."

"No; my apostles were already chosen beforehand. He could have entered into a relationship with me, having the saving grace of my Father and receiving life's blessings. I would have mentored him and brought him to my Father's will, allowing him to store up wonderful treasure in heaven. He would have had my protection from this world."

Or let him take hold of my strength, that he may make peace with me, and he shall make peace with Me.

Isaiah 27:5 (KJV)

"I am here for anyone who wants a relationship with me."

That if you *confess with your mouth Jesus as Lord*, and believe in your heart that God raised Him from the dead, you will be saved for with the heart a person believes, resulting in righteousness, and *with the mouth* he confesses, *resulting in salvation*.

Romans 10:9–10

If this is something you would like to do, contact your local Christian church or email me: Jesuschrist@Joshuabusiness. com or www.joshuabusiness.com

Larry A. Brown Sr.

Find a church that believes in the Bible as the authority in Word, focuses on Jesus Christ as the only begotten Son of God, and holds to the unwavering truth that Jesus is the only way to the Father. They will lead you in this wonderful experience, transforming your life forever!

"I am here and I am waiting for you!"

"My choice to move my people in this next section was with Abram from the bloodline of Shem, Noah's son. Let's go there."

> Now the Lord said to Abram, "Go forth from your country, and from your relatives and from your father's house, to the land which I will show you; and I will make you a great nation, and I will bless you, and make your name great; and so you shall be a blessing; and I will bless those who bless you, and the one who curses you I will curse, and in you all the families of the earth will be blessed."
>
> Genesis 12:1–3

"That is a lot of blessing bestowed on one man, isn't it?"

"It is not only for him; the blessing came upon him because of his seed."

> Now to Abraham *and his seed* where the promises made.
>
> Galatians 3:16 (KJV)

"He does not say, 'And to seeds,' as referring too many, but rather to one, *'And to your seed,'* that is, *Christ.*"

"So what you are saying is that the blessing on Abram was put there for the world to receive your Son?"

"Yes! That is the blessing."

"Then I commanded Abram to go forth from his relatives."

"Yes, Lord, but why did Abram take Lot? You told him to go without his relatives. Wasn't Lot his nephew? Lot caused a lot of problems for Abraham, didn't he?"

"Yes, he did."

> And there was strife between the herdsmen of Abram's livestock and the herdsmen of Lot's livestock. Now the Canaanite and the Perizzite were in the land. So Abram said to Lot, "Please let there be no strife between you and me, nor between my herdsmen and your herdsmen, for we are brothers. Is not the whole land before you? Please separate from me; if to the left, then I will go to the right; or if to the right then I will go to the left." So Lot chose for himself all the valley of the Jordan, and Lot journeyed eastward. Thus they separated from each other. Abram settled in the land of Canaan, while Lot settled in the cities of the valley, and moved his tents as far as Sodom. *Now the men of Sodom were wicked exceedingly and sinners against the* LORD.
>
> Genesis 13:7–9, 11–13

"That looks like trouble. Why would anyone move into an area in that condition?"

"The covenant was given to Abram, not to Lot. I never spoke to Lot, and the relationship wasn't with him. When Lot left, look what happened."

> The Lord said to Abram, after Lot had separated from him, "Lift up now thine eyes and look from the place where though art northward and southward and eastward and westward; *for all the land which thou seeth, I will give it and to thy seed forever.*
>
> Genesis 13:14–15 (KJV)

"I chose the bloodline of the seed of Abraham, not Lot. People can make their own choices, but I will continue with my plan.

"As you will see, Abram's decision to not listen to me and leave Lot at home has consequences in the world.

"After I destroyed Sodom, Lot went into the mountains with his two daughters."

"I know what happened here. This is where the daughters of Lot thought there were no men left on the earth, so they got their father drunk and had children by him, right?"

"Right."

> Thus both the daughters of Lot were with child by their father. The firstborn bore a son, and called his name *Moab;* he is the father of the *Moabites* to this day. As for the younger, she also bore a son, and called his name Ben-ammi; he is the father of the sons of *Ammon* to this day.
>
> Genesis 19:36–38

> No *Ammonite* or *Moabite shall enter the assembly of the Lord, none of their descendants*, even to the tenth generation, shall ever enter into the assembly of the Lord.
>
> Deuteronomy 23:3

On that day they read aloud from the book of Moses in the hearing of the people; and there was found written in it that no *Ammonite or Moabite* should ever enter the assembly of God, because they did not meet the sons of Israel with bread and water, but hired Balaam against them *to curse* them. *However, our God turned the curse into a blessing.*

Nehemiah 13:1–2

"Wow! This all happened because Abram didn't follow the rules?"

"Yes. To this day, the Ammonites and the Moabites are causing trouble for the descendants of Shem."

"So this is what we've got so far. Ham messed up; he is the Father of the Canaanites, a servant of servants to Shem's descendants, right?"

"Right."

"Lot's daughters did what they did, knowing that there was a city named Zoar right there. Their offspring became the Ammonites and the Moabites, which *cursed* the sons of Israel, right?"

"Right."

"What about the third son of Noah: Japheth? Who were his sons?"

The sons of Japheth; *Gomer* and *Magog* and Madai and Javan and *Tubal* and *Meshech* and Tiras.

Genesis 10:2 (KJV)

And a word of the LORD came to me saying, "Son of man, set your face against *Gog* the land of *Magog,*

Larry A. Brown Sr.

the chief prince of Meshech and *Tubal*, and prophesy against him and say, 'Thus says the Lord God, "Behold, I am against thee, *O Gog, the chief Prince of Meshech and Tubal.*"

Ezekiel 38:1–3 (KJV)

Gomer, and all his bands; the house of Togarmah (Sons of Gomer), from the north quarters and all its bands and many people with thee.

Ezekiel 38:6 (KJV)

"These are the people that have a problem with Israel; they are all related! Why?"

"I am the God of Abraham, Isaac, and Jacob."

Then the word of the Lord came to me, saying, "Son of man, your brothers, your relatives, your fellow exiles and the whole house of Israel, all of them, *are those to whom the inhabitants of Jerusalem have said*, 'Go far from the Lord; this land has been given us as a possession.'

"Lord, the people talking here are not Israelites right?"

"Right!"

"The inhabitants of Jerusalem are trying to intimidate my chosen from returning to the land and following their rightful path."

Therefore say, 'Thus says the Lord God, though I had removed them *(Israelites)* far away among the nations and though I had scattered them *(Israelites)* among the countries, yet I was a sanctuary for them a little while in the countries where they had gone."

> Therefore say, 'Thus says the Lord God, I will gather you from the peoples and assemble you out of the countries among which you have been scattered, and *I will give you the land of Israel."*
>
> Ezekiel 11:14–17

"So this is all about the land?"
    "Yes, but not just that."

> When they come there, they will remove all its detestable things and all its abominations from it. And I will give them one heart, and *put a new spirit within them.* And I will take the heart of stone out of their flesh and give them a heart of flesh, that they may walk in my statutes and keep My ordinances and do them. Then *they will be my people, and I shall be their God.*
>
> Ezekiel 11:18–20

"It is all about my blessings to my chosen people."

> Ye worship ye know not what: we know what we worship: for salvation is of the Jews.
>
> John 4:22 (KJV)

"Those that hear my call can join me through my son, Jesus Christ, or they can fight me; the choice is theirs. I am the God of Abraham, Isaac, and Jacob."
    "Wow! I choose you! Not from fear but from choice. I made this choice many years ago and have had a loving relationship with your Son ever since."

> Because ye are sons, God has sent forth the Spirit of his Son into your hearts, crying, "Abba Father!"

Galatians 4:6 (KJV)

"When I became a Christian, I had no idea of how to start or what to do. Was I supposed to go to church every day as I saw some do? Was I supposed to give all my money away and feed the poor? Was I supposed to join the Peace Corps and travel the world?"

"How could you? You had no understanding of the guidance of my son. You never looked at the Bible for any help. When you got 'the feeling to do something,' you reacted with no consideration of the ramifications on others. You found out very quickly this was wrong, bringing you to an unhappy, psychotic mindset. You looked to people and their answers, trying to survive this world with no luck, furthering this frustrating mindset! I sent my people to help you. Remember your grandmother taking you to church when you were a young man? When you finally got to church, you were thinking how stupid it was! Your next step in looking for the truth found yourself reading books, searching for my power, finding that searching for me without the Bible as your reference was very dangerous. On and on and on you went without any understanding. Then there was the time—"

"Okay, let's cut to the chase! This is what God showed me as a young Christian."

I could feel his gentle smile on my heart as I continued.

"You must start with the understanding that you know nothing and need a relationship with the one who knows everything."

"Sounds good so far!"

"This is extremely difficult these days; everyone knows everything in this world. You will find out!"

"Slow down! You're a little uneasy."

"Okay. You're right! Ask to have a relationship with Jesus; you have the right to do this."

"My Father sent his Spirit into your heart when you accepted me as your Savior."

"This relationship will have you looking into what the Bible really has to say, conferring with him on what his words are revealing to your heart."

"I will guide you into the Father's will for you."

"Consider doing it right now and save the embarrassment that I went through. In my opinion, the worst thing you can do is take someone else's interpretation of what the Bible is saying for you."

"Really? Why would you do that?"

"Listening and studying with your pastor, discussions with your Christian friends, communicating about the Word is essential in your walk, but solely relying on their interpretation would not be wise. Opening your mind to the Bible and allowing our relationship to grown in that knowledge will guide you through all things."

"Take *The God Walking Program,* for instance; read it with the help of Jesus for your understanding. Having a relationship with the God of the universe, we must be able to speak his language. His language is his word: the Bible."

> For by these He has granted to us His precious and magnificent promises, so that by them *you may become partakers of the divine nature,* having escaped the corruption that is in the world by lust. Now for this very reason also, applying all diligence, in your faith supply moral excellence, and in your *moral excellence,* knowledge, and in your *knowledge,* self-control, and in your *self-control,* perseverance, and in your *perseverance,* godliness, and in your *godliness,* brotherly kindness, and in your *brotherly kindness, love.* For if these qualities are yours and are increasing, they render you neither useless nor unfruitful in the true knowledge of our Lord Jesus Christ.
>
> 2 Peter 1:4–8

Until we understand that we must have a relationship with Jesus Christ to understand the prompting of the Holy Spirit within us (by his word) we will never grow into the Father's will; or grow, period!

Section 7: Abram's Son, Ishmael

And Abram said, "Since you have given no offspring to me, one born in my house is my heir." Then behold, the word of the Lord came to him, saying, "This man will not be your heir; but one who will come forth from your own body, he shall be your heir."

Genesis 15:3–4

Now Sarai, Abram's wife bare him no children, and she had a handmaid, an Egyptian whose name was Hagar.

Genesis 16:1 (KJV)

"This sounds like trouble to me, doesn't it?"

"Remember the situation with Lot and what happened? Abram is doing it again."

> And Sarai said unto Abram, Behold now, the LORD hath restrained me from bearing: I pray thee, go in unto my maid; it may be that I may obtain children by her. And Abram hearkened to the voice of Sarai.
>
> Genesis 16:2 (KJV)

"This sounds like what happened when Eve gave Adam the fruit in the Garden."

"It does, and you will see the consequence."

> He went into Hagar, and she conceived; and when she saw that she had conceived, her mistress was despised in her sight. But Abram said to Sarai, "Behold, your maid is in your power; do to her what is good in your sight." So Sarai treated her harshly, and she fled from her presence. Now the angel of the Lord found her by a spring of water in the wilderness, by the spring on the way to Shur. He said, "Hagar, Sarai's maid, where have you come from and where are you going?" And she said, "I am fleeing from the presence of my mistress Sarai." Then the angel of the Lord said to her, "Return to your mistress, and submit yourself to her authority." Moreover, the angel of the LORD said to her, *"I will greatly multiply your descendants* so that they will be too many to count." The angel of the Lord said to her further, "Behold, you are with child, and you will bear a son; and you shall call his name Ishmael, because the LORD has given heed to your affliction. He will be a wild donkey of a man, his hand will be

Larry A. Brown Sr.

against everyone, and everyone's hand will be against him; *and he will live to the east of all his brothers."*

Genesis 16:4, 6–12

"Wow! That must have hurt. You said this to a mother-to-be?"

"Yes, this was hard for her. Remember, though, I multiply her descendants. Ishmael was a different story; he came from Abram's seed."

> And Abraham said to God, "Oh *that Ishmael* might live before you!" But God said, *"No, but Sarah your wife will bear a son,* and you shall call his name Isaac; and I will establish my covenant with him for an everlasting covenant for his descendants after him. As for Ishmael, I have heard you; behold, I will bless him, and will make him fruitful and will multiply him exceedingly. He shall become the father of twelve princes [Captain or Chief], and I will make him a great nation.
>
> Genesis 17:18–20

"So you are saying that Ishmael's bloodline became a great nation. What nation did they become, Iraq or Iran?"

"Neither. Let me explain, and you will see what happened."

> Now these are the records of the generations of Ishmael, Abraham's son, whom Hagar the Egyptian, Sarah's maid, bore to Abraham; and these are the names of the sons of Ishmael, by their names, by the order of their birth: (12 Princes) Nebaioth, Kedar,

Adbeel, Mibsam, Mishma, Dumah, Massa, Hadad, Tema, Jetur, Naphish, Kedemah. These are the sons of Ishmael and these are their names, by their villages, and by their camps; twelve princes [Captain or Chief] according to their tribes. These are the years of the life of Ishmael, one hundred and thirty-seven years; and he breathed his last and *died, and was gathered to his people.* They settled from *Havilah to Shur which is east of Egypt as one goes toward Assyria;* he settled in defiance of all his relatives.

Genesis 25:12–15

"Isn't that the same place that King Saul was sent to by Samuel the prophet to destroy all who lived there?"

"Let's take a look. Go to 1 Samuel 15:3."

Now go and strike Amalek and utterly destroy all that they have, and spare them not; but slay both man and woman, infant and suckling, ox and sheep, camel and ass …

So Saul smote the Amalekites, *from Havilah until thou comest to Shur that is over against Egypt.*

1 Samuel 15:3, 7 (KJV)

"That is the same place where the Ishmaelites lived, right?"

"Right."

And the Lord sent thee on a journey, and said, "Go and utterly destroy the sinners, the Amalekites, and fight against them until they be consumed."

1 Samuel 15:18 (KJV)

Larry A. Brown Sr.

"So what you are saying is that King Saul destroyed all the people of this area?"

"Not all; go to verses five and six."

> Saul came to the city of Amalek and set an ambush in the valley. Saul said to the Kenites [Ham's descendants], "Go, depart, go down from among the Amalekites, *so that I do not destroy you with them*; for you showed kindness to all the sons of Israel when they came up from Egypt." So the Kenites departed from among the Amalekites.

"So God saved the Kenites because they were not an enemy of Saul. What about the Ishmaelites in the area?"

> For they have conspired together with one mind; against you [God] they make a covenant: The tents of Edom [Esau] and the *Ishmaelites*, Moab and the Hagrites: Gebal and Ammon and *Amalek*, Philistia, with the inhabitants of Tyre.
>
> Psalm 83:5

"The writer of this psalm was reviewing what had happened and what was going to happen."

"So Saul destroyed the Amalekites (Esau's grandson) and all the people in the area except the Kenites?"

"Yes."

"So this is why one of the present day religions has forbidden their people from going back in their genealogy past a stated number of generations, because their prophet could not find his way back to Ishmael?"

"The Holy Spirit has revealed this to you."

"So was this the end of Ishmael's descendants?"

"Not all."

> Now Esau saw that Isaac had blessed Jacob and
> sent him away to Paddan-aram to take to himself
> a wife from there, and that when he blessed him,
> he charged him, saying, "You shall not take a wife
> from the daughters of Canaan," So Esau saw that
> the daughters of Canaan displeased his father Isaac;
> and Esau went to Ishmael and married, besides the
> wives that he had, *Mahalath the daughter of Ishmael*,
> Abraham's son, the sister of Nebaioth.
>
> Genesis 28:6, 8–9

"So if this present-day religion would trace their ancestries back, they would find Esau, Jacob's twin brother!"

"The Holy Spirit has revealed this to you."

"Wow! But all this talk about Ishmael doesn't really mean much in the Father's will, does it?"

"No, it doesn't. The real problem in this world is the land and the blessing that comes with it. This is the land I promised to my chosen ones: Abraham, Isaac, and Jacob.

> On that day the Lord made a covenant with Abram,
> saying, "To your descendants I have given this land,
> from the river of Egypt [Nile] as far as the great river,
> the river Euphrates [Iraq].
>
> Genesis 15:18

"That's the entire Middle East."

Larry A. Brown Sr.

"Now you see! It's all about my covenant with Abraham, Isaac, and Jacob—the land equally important! It's all about my covenant with my son."

Salvation to the Gentiles

Section 8: Abraham's Son, Isaac

"Isaac is an interesting character wasn't he Lord?"
"Let's take a look."

> And the LORD visited Sarah as he had said, and the
> LORD did unto Sarah as he had spoken.
>
> Genesis 21:1 (KJV)

> I will bless her [Sarah] and give thee [Abraham] a
> son also of her. yea I will bless her, and she shall be a
> mother of nations; kings of people shall be of her.
>
> Genesis 17:16 (KJV)

> 2For Sarah conceived, and bare Abraham a son in his old age, at the set time of which God had spoken to him. 3And Abraham called the name of his son that was born unto him, whom Sarah bare to him, Isaac.
>
> Genesis 21:2–3 (KJV)

"My choice for my covenant was with Isaac."

"I can see that, but what was the deal with Abraham taking Isaac to be offered as a burnt offering to you in Genesis 22:1?"

"I was testing Abraham."

"Tested?"

"Yes, 'tested.' Abraham had shown me that he had the ability to make bad choices by adding his thoughts to my blessings and then acting on them. Now I will show you a prophetic vision of my truth! Take a look."

> He said, "Take now thy son, *thine only son Isaac,* whom *thou lovest,* Isaac, and get thee into the *land of Moriah*, and offer him there for a burnt offering upon one of the *mountains which I will tell thee of.*"
>
> Genesis 22:2 (KJV)

> Isaac spoke to Abraham his father and said, "My father!" And he said, "Here I am, my son." And he said, "Behold, the fire and the wood, but where is the lamb for the burnt offering?" Abraham said, "God will provide for *Himself the lamb* for the burnt offering, my son" So the two of them walked on together.
>
> Genesis 22:7–8

Larry A. Brown Sr.

"Is this talking about Isaac or you? The verse says, 'Your only son,' but Abraham had Ishmael *and* Isaac. Are you showing us that this was about you and what God was going to do, that he was going *to send his only Son,* the one *that he loved,* as a sacrifice for all of us?"

"Look at 2 Chronicles 3:1."

> Then Solomon began to build the house of the Lord in Jerusalem on Mount Moriah, where the Lord had appeared to his father David, at the place that David had prepared on the threshing floor of Ornan the Jebusite.
>
> 2 Chronicles 3:1

"You prepared this place for yourself through Abraham when you commanded Abraham to sacrifice his only son. You provided the lamb in yourself, right?"

"You are right! I am the lamb!"

> Abraham stretched out his hand and took the knife to slay his son. But the angel of the Lord called to him from heaven and said, "Abraham, Abraham!" And he said, "Here I am." He said, "Do not stretch out your hand against the lad, and do nothing to him; for now I know that you fear GOD, since you *have not withheld your son, your only son* from Me. Abraham called the name of that place, The LORD will Provide, as it is said to this day, "In the mount of the LORD it will be provided."
>
> Genesis 22:10–12, 14

> And Isaac was forty years old when he took Rebekah, the daughter of Bethuel the Aramean of Paddan-

aram, the sister of Laban the Aramean, to be his wife. Isaac prayed to the Lord on behalf of his wife, because she was barren; and the Lord answered him and Rebekah his wife conceived.

Genesis 25:20–21

"Lord, why were both Abraham's wife, Sarah, and Isaac's wife, Rebekah, barren? This had to be your hand, because it is hard for me to believe that they would go throughout an entire area searching for a wife for Isaac only to pick a barren woman."

"Yes, it was by my hand and my will."

> He [Abraham] said to me [Abraham's servant], "The Lord, before whom I have walked, will send His angel with you to make your journey successful, and you will take a wife for my son from my relatives and from my father's house."
>
> So I came today to a spring, and said, "O Lord, the GOD of my master Abraham, if now You will make my journey on which I go successful; behold, I am standing by the spring, and may it be that the maiden who comes out to draw, and to whom I say, 'Please let me drink a little water from your jar;' and she [Rebekah] will say to me, 'You drink, and I will draw for your camels also'; let her be the woman whom the Lord has appointed for my master's son."
>
> Then they called Rebekah and said to her, "will you go with this man?" And she said, "I will go." Thus they sent away their sister Rebekah and her nurse with Abraham's servant and his men.

Genesis 24:40, 42–44, 58–59

"You are in full control no matter what we do?"

"Yes, I am! By having a relationship with my Son, trusting that we know what we're doing, you will achieve the purpose in my will. If you choose *not to*, then we will send you back to the beginning until you see it while you try to fulfill the yearnings of your heart, or I will take you home not achieving it."

"Wow! I wouldn't want to have to tell you why I didn't trust you enough to achieve your will in my life."

"Sadly, I hear it all the time! Continue with Rebekah in Genesis 25, verses 22–23."

"Okay."

> But the children struggled together within her; and she said, "If it is so, why then am I this way?" So she went to inquire of the Lord. The Lord said to her, "Two nations are in your womb; and two peoples will be separated from your body; and one people shall be stronger than the other; and the older shall serve the younger."

"What two nations are you talking about?"

"Israel (Isaac); Edom (Esau)."

> Then the Lord stirred up *an adversary* unto Solomon, *Hadad the Edomite*; he was *of the king's seed in Edom* (tribe of Esau).
>
> 1 Kings 11:14 (KJV)

"Why, Lord, did you raise up an adversary to Solomon?"

Now King Solomon loved many strange women together with the daughter of Pharaoh; women of the Moabite, Ammonite, *Edomite*, Sidonian, and Hittite, of the nations concerning which the Lord had said unto the children of Israel, "Ye shall not go in to them, neither shall they come in unto you, for surely they will turn away your heart after their gods:" Solomon clave unto these in love.

1 Kings 11:1–2 (KJV)

"Wow! Let's see what happens."

For it came about, when David was in Edom, and Joab the commander of the army had gone up to bury the slain, and had struck down every male in Edom for Joab and all Israel stayed there six months, until he had cut off every male in Edom (tribe of Esau). *That Hadad* fled to Egypt, he and certain Edomites of his father's servants with him, while Hadad was a young boy.

God also raised up *another adversary* to him, Rezon the son of Eliada, who had fled for the lord Hadadezer king of Zobah. He gathered men to himself and became leader of a marauding band, after David slew them of Zobah; and they went to *Damascus* (Syria) and stayed there, and reigned in Damascus. So he was an *adversary* to Israel all the days of Solomon, along with *the evil that Hadad* did; and he abhorred Israel and reigned over Aram.

1 Kings 11:15–17, 23–25

"You keep saying *adversary* in these texts. Wasn't that the name of *Satan* in the Old Testament?"

"Yes, it was!"

"The word *adversary* used here in this text actually means *Satan*, doesn't it?"

"Yes, it does! Now, let's talk about my chosen one, Jacob.

> Then Jacob departed from Beersheba and went toward Haran. He came to a certain place and spent the night there, because the sun had set; and he took one of the stones of the place and put it under his head, and lay down in that place. He had a dream, and behold, a ladder was set on the earth with its top reaching heaven; and behold, the angels of GOD were ascending and descending on it. And behold, the LORD stood above it and said, "I am the Lord, the GOD of your father Abraham and the GOD of Isaac; *the land* on which you lie, *I will give it to you* and to your descendants."
>
> Genesis 28:10–13

"As you can see, it is all about the land and the blessing I placed on my children."

"Wow!"

"Yes, it is. Let's take a look at Jacob. Write down the sons of Jacob."

"Okay."

From his wife, Leah:
- Reuben
- Simeon
- Levi
- Judah
- Issachar
- Zebulun

From Rachel's maid, Bilhah:
- Dan
- Naphtali

From Leah's maid, Zilpah:
- Gad
- Asher

From his wife, Rachel:
- Joseph
- Benjamin

Now you can see Abraham, Isaac, and Jacob as the chosen bloodline. There is so much in the Old Testament that shows us the development of the prophetic nature toward Our Lord and Savior and the will of God.

Section 9: From the Tribe of Judah

1And it came to pass at that time, that Judah went down from his brethren, and turned in to a certain Adullamite, whose name was Hirah.

2And Judah saw there a daughter of a certain Canaanite, whose name was Shuah; and he took her, and went in unto her.

Genesis 38:1–2 (KJV)

"Here we go again!"

She conceived and bares a son and he called his

name Er. And she conceived again and bare a son and she called his name Onan and she yet conceived and bare a son and called his name Shelah; and he was at Chezib when she bare him. And Judah took a wife for Er his firstborn, whose name was Tamar. And Er, Judah's firstborn, was wicked in the sight of the Lord, and the Lord slew him.

Genesis 38:3–7 (KJV)

"Wow! He must have been a really bad person!"

"He was. But this saga hasn't ended. If only people would just follow my directions. My word is there for all to see. By following my word, you will be protected and blessed."

"I am sorry that your people cannot see that."

"Me too!"

Then Judah said to Onan, "Go into your brother's wife, and perform your duty as a brother-in-law to her, and raise up offspring for your brother."

Genesis 38:8

"What does that mean?"

It shall be that the firstborn whom she bears shall assume the name of the dead brother, so that his name will not be blotted out from Israel.

But if the man does not desire to take his brother's wife, then his brother's wife shall go up to the gate to the elders and say, "My husband's brother refuses to establish a name for his brother in Israel; he is not willing to perform the duty of a husband's brother to me." Then the elders of his city shall summon him

Larry A. Brown Sr.

and speak to him. And if he persists and says, "I do not desire to take her," then his brother's wife shall come to him in the sight of the elders, and pull his sandal off of his foot and spit in his face; and she shall declare, "Thus it is done to the man who does not build up his brother's house."

Deuteronomy 25:6–9

"This was very important in that culture, wasn't it?"

"It was all about the bloodline, and it still is. After knowing how important the bloodline was, look what Onan does."

Onan knew that the offspring would be not his; so when he went in to his brother's wife, he wasted his seed on the ground in order not to give offspring to his brother.

Genesis 38:9

"This did not make you happy, did it?"

And the thing which he did displeased the Lord; wherefore he slew him also.

Genesis 38:10 (KJV)

After listening to what God had just said, I felt something inside of me cry out! My heart was beating faster as I lifted up my hands and gave thanks. Thanking him for the opportunity to have a relationship with his Son, Jesus Christ, guiding and protecting me. Thank you, Father God!

"You are welcome."

> Ask, and it shall be given you; seek, and ye shall find; knock, and it shall be opened unto you:
> 8For every one that asketh receiveth; and he that seeketh findeth; and to him that knocketh it shall be opened.
>
> Mathew 7:7–8 (KJV)

Let's continue. Go to Genesis 38:11.

> Then Judah said to his daughter-in-law Tamar, "Remain a widow in your father's house until my son Shelah grows up"; for he thought, *I am afraid that he too may die like his brothers.* So Tamar went and lived in her father's house.
>
> Genesis 38:11

"Lord, why didn't he go to you for help on this instead of blaming Tamar?"

"This is the age-old story; my people are trying to come up with their answers by themselves instead of seeking me for help. Seek and you will find! I am always here, always! Tamar finally had children. She had twins—one was named Perez and the other was Zerah. I want you to guess who the father was."

"Shelah, Judah's son," I said with confidence.

"I see you were listening. Let's take a look."

Hearing him say that made my heart smile!

> Now it was about three months later that Judah was informed, "Your daughter-in-law Tamar has

Larry A. Brown Sr.

played a harlot, and behold, she is also with child by harlotry." Then Judah said, "Bring her out and let her be burned!"

Genesis 38:24

I was not smiling anymore! "I was obviously wrong on the father, right?"

"Right!"

> It was while she was being brought out that she sent to her father-in-law, saying, "I am with child by the man to whom these things belong." And she said, "Please examine and see, whose signet ring and cords and staff are these?" Judah recognized them, and said, "She is more righteous than I, inasmuch as I did not give her to my son Shelah." *And he did not have relations with her again.*

Genesis 38:25–26

"The father was Judah!"

"Yes, he was. My children have found ways to reject my help and my protection. Even though this happens a lot, my will continues. Tamar's child was Perez, continuing the bloodline of Judah to my Son. Judah, by not following my directions, was unequally yoked with his Canaanite wife. This caused all types of problems for him. My will with the chosen ones will continue with or without their help. As in David, he did not get to build the temple, but my will was done. As in Moses, he did not go into the promised land, but my will was done. I have chosen you for a particular situation, and it will get done, dragging you kicking and screaming or blessing and honoring me. The choice is yours. Let's continue.

"There was a famine in the area where Jacob was living. I sent Jacob and his family to Egypt with the favor of the pharaoh of Egypt. This happened after the sons of Jacob sold their brother, Joseph, to a wandering group of people."

"Why would they do that?"

"Guess the person who had the idea to sell him."

"Who?"

"Let's take a look and see."

> Judah [Him again!] said to his brothers, "What profit is it for us to kill our brother and cover up his blood? Come let us sell him to the Ishmaelites and not lay our hands on him, for he is our brother, our own flesh. And his brothers listened to him. Then some Midianite traders passed by, so they pulled him up and lifted Joseph out of the pit, and sold him to the Ishmaelites for twenty shekels of silver. Thus they brought Joseph into Egypt...
>
> Meanwhile, the Midianites sold him in Egypt to Potiphar, Pharaoh's officer, the captain of the bodyguard.
>
> Genesis 37:26–28, 36

> The Lord was with Joseph and he was a successful man. And he was in the house of his master, the Egyptian.
>
> Genesis 39:2 (NKJV)

> Pharaoh also said to Joseph, "I am Pharaoh, and without your consent no man may lift his hand or foot in all the land of Egypt."
>
> Genesis 41:44 (NKJV)

Larry A. Brown Sr.

But now do not therefore be grieved or angry with yourselves because you sold me here, for God sent me before you to preserve life.

Genesis 45:5 (NKJV)

"Joseph understood God's will for his life."

"Lord, wouldn't it be nice if we all could understand and forgive like Joseph?"

"Yes, it is essential that you do!"

God *sent me* before you *to preserve* posterity for you in the earth; and to save your *lives by a great deliverance.* So now, it was not you who sent me here, but God; and He has made me a father to Pharaoh and lord of his house and a ruler throughout all the land of Egypt.

Genesis 45:7–8 (NKJV)

"I am in control and always will be!"

"I understand!"

"List the names of the sons of Jacob that *I took out of Egypt.*"

"Okay."

- The sons of Reuben
- The sons of Simeon
- The son of Levi
- The sons of Judah
- The sons of Issachar
- The sons of Zebulun
- The sons of Gad
- The sons of Asher

- The sons of Dan
- The sons of Naphtali
- The sons of Benjamin

"What about the sons of Joseph: Ephraim, and Manasseh, for Israel (Jacob) had blessed them?"

> Then *Jacob said to Joseph,* "God almighty appeared to me at Luz in the land of Canaan and blessed me, and He said to me, 'Behold I will make you fruitful and numerous, and I will make you a company of peoples, and will give you this land to your descendents after you for an everlasting possession.' *Now your two sons,* who were born to you in the land of Egypt, *are mine; Ephraim and Manasseh* shall be mine, as Rueben and Simeon are. But your offspring that have been born after them are yours.
>
> Genesis 48:3–6

"So to save your people, you sent Joseph ahead *to preserve* and to keep them *alive for a great deliverance.* They were the direct descendants of Jacob, right?"

"Right. Now once again you can see it is all about the blood of the chosen ones."

"I am starting to get the picture. You are personally guiding us through the stories of your chosen people and their choices in life. We're seeing their interaction with their God, or their lack of it. This gives us a very important understanding that you are in control and you are using us in assisting your will. You will protect and bless us for understanding this reality. We have a loving Father who is calling us out of the darkness of this world. Receiving

Larry A. Brown Sr.

this call is the greatest experience of this lifetime—nothing else matters! By accepting the call from the Father, we move into another dimension of life. This dimension leads us through his Son straight into our Father's arms."

Section 10: The Triune Spirit of God

1. God the Father
2. God the Son
3. God the Holy Spirit

> For from Him and through Him and to Him are all things. To Him be the Glory forever. Amen.
>
> Romans 11:36

"Lord, can you show us what we have to do to get into these dimensions of God? How we can grow into a relationship with you, guiding us to the Father's will?"

For God so loved the world that He gave His only begotten Son, that *whoever believeth in Him* should not perish, but have everlasting life.

John 3:16 (KJV)

I am the door; by me *if any man enter in, he shall be saved,* and shall go in and out and find pasture.

John 10:9 (KJV)

That if you confess with your mouth Jesus as Lord and believe in your heart that GOD raised Him from the dead, you will be saved; for with the heart a person believes, resulting in righteousness, and with *the mouth he confesses, resulting in salvation.*

Romans 10:9–10

"I want you to notice that there are two completely different statements written in Romans 10:9."

"What two statements are you referring to?"

"Part one: If you confess with your mouth; Part two: And believe with your heart. Conclusion: You will be saved."

"That is what we have to do to be saved, right?"

"Wrong."

"What do you mean?"

"Romans 10:10. Part one: For with the heart a person believes, *resulting in righteousness.* Part two: And with the mouth he confesses, *resulting in salvation.* One of the biggest problems my people have in this world today is they think that they have to come to me in perfect condition and completely understand me before they can be saved. You can only find my Father's will through Me."

Larry A. Brown Sr.

Whoever therefore shall confess Me before men, him will I confess also before My Father which is in heaven.

Matthew 10:32 (KJV)

For by thy words thou shalt be justified and by thy words thou shalt be condemned.

Matthew 12:37 (KJV)

For the Son of Man is come to seek and to save that which was lost.

Luke 19:10 (KJV)

One of the criminals who were hanged there was hurling abuse at Him, saying, "Are you not the Christ? Save yourself and us!" But the other answered, and rebuking him said, "Do you not even fear God, since you are under the same sentence of condemnation? And we indeed are suffering justly, for we are receiving what we deserve for our deeds; but this man has done nothing wrong." And he was saying, "Jesus, remember me when You come into Your kingdom!" And He said, "Truly I say to you, today you shall be with me in Paradise."

Luke 23:39–43

"So he couldn't have possibly known about the resurrection because it had not happened yet, right?"

"Right! My people think it is so complicated to be saved, but it isn't. Just be obedient to the call from my Father and confess with your mouth that I am Lord. Then he will send His Holy Spirit into your heart and you are saved. That is all you have to do! The heart will grow as our relationship grows."

> And hope does not disappoint, because the love of God has been poured out within our hearts through the Holy Spirit who was given to us.
>
> Romans 5:5

> My sheep hear My voice, and I know them, and they follow Me; and I give onto them eternal life, and they shall never perish; neither shall any man pluck them out of My hand.
>
> John 10:27–28 (KJV)

> But He, having offered one sacrifice for sins for all time, sat down at the right hand of God, waiting from that time onward until His enemies be made a footstool for His feet. For by one offering He has perfected for all time those who are sanctified. And the Holy Spirit also testifies to us; for after saying, "This is the covenant that I will make with them after those days, says the Lord: I will put My laws upon their heart, and on their mind I will write them." He then says, "And their sins and their lawless deeds I will remember no more."
>
> Hebrews 10:12–17

"Now we know how to be saved. What happens next?"

> However, you are not in the flesh but in the Spirit, if indeed *the Spirit of* GOD *[Holy Spirit] dwells in you.* But if anyone does not have the *Spirit of Christ*, he does not belong to Him.
>
> Romans 8:9

Larry A. Brown Sr.

"This is another two-part answer, isn't it?"

"Yes. By seeing this you are starting to understand.

"This means that once you accept my call and accept the Son, I will send My Holy Spirit into your heart. By your acceptance, you have completed your salvation requirements and you are saved. Now you must choose to have a relationship with my Son allowing his Spirit to enter you.

> But he that is joined unto the Lord is one spirit.
>
> 1 Corinthians 6:17 (KJV)

> Therefore as you have received Christ Jesus the Lord, so walk in Him, having been firmly rooted and now being built up in Him and established in your faith, just as you were instructed, and overflowing with gratitude.
>
> Colossians 2:6

> Therefore if you have been raised up with Christ, keep seeking the things above, where Christ is, seated at the right hand of GOD. Set your mind on the things above, not on things that are on earth. For you have died and *your life is hidden with Christ in* GOD.
>
> Colossians 3:1–3

> Do not lie to one another, since you laid aside the old self with its evil practices, and have put on the new self who is being renewed to a true knowledge according to the image of the One who created him.
>
> Colossians 3:9–10

> And do not be conformed to this world, but be transformed by the renewing of your mind, so that

you may prove what the *will* of God is, that which is good and acceptable and perfect.

Romans 12:2

Therefore we have been buried with Him through baptism into death, so that as Christ was raised from the dead through the glory of the Father, so we too might walk in newness of life.

Romans 6:4

In that day you will know that I am in My Father and you in Me, and I in you.

John 14:20

"Once you ask for this relationship, my Son, in conjunction with the Holy Spirit, will guide you into my will."

But if the *Spirit of Him who raised Jesus from the dead* dwells in you, He who raised Christ Jesus from the dead will also give life to your mortal bodies through His Spirit who dwells in you.

Romans 8:11

Jesus answered and said to him, "If anyone loves Me he will keep My word; and My father will love him and *we* will come to him and make Our abode [residence] with him.

John 14:23

"So what you are saying is that to grow into the Father's will, we must first confess with our mouth that your Son is our Savior?"

"Right!"

> For by thy words thou shalt be justified and by thy words thou shalt be condemned.
>
> Matthew 12:37 (KJV)

"Then we must choose to have a relationship with him, right?"

"Right!"

> Therefore we do not lose heart, but though our outer man is decaying, our inner man is being renewed day by day.
>
> 2 Corinthians 4:16

"What is next?"

"Then *we* come and abide in you."

"Wow! How does that happen?"

"Love."

> He that loveth not knoweth not God, for God is love.
>
> 1 John 4:8 (KJV)

"You must understand that you loving me is not enough to get to the Father's will. In your relationship with me, you will come to the understanding that Abba loves you personally!"

> We love, *because He first loved us.*
>
> 1 John 4:19

"To help you understand this, we need to go to the beginning and look at the law. Understanding the law is the key that unlocks the mystery of the saving grace of the Father."

Doing my will is doing my work.

Section 11: From the Tribe of Levi

Now these are the names of the children of Israel which came into Egypt every man and his household came with Jacob.

Exodus 1:1–4 (KJV)

"Verses 2–4; list the names."

1. Reuben
2. Simeon
3. Levi
4. Judah

5. Issachar
6. Zebulun
7. Benjamin
8. Dan
9. Naphtali
10. Gad
11. Asher

> All the souls that came out of the loins of Jacob were seventy souls, for Joseph was in Egypt already. Joseph died, and all his brothers and all that generation.
>
> Exodus 1:5–6 (KJV)

"These are the same people you sent Joseph to Egypt for? These are also the same people that sold him in the first place, starting this process?"

"I took their unwilling hearts and protected the bloodline of my chosen one, preserving their lives and keeping them alive for the great deliverance in Genesis 45:5. I am in control. It's all about the blood."

> But the sons of Israel were fruitful and increased greatly, and multiplied, and became exceedingly mighty, so that the land was filled with them. Now the new king arose over Egypt who did not know Joseph. He said to his people, "Behold, the people of the sons of Israel are more and mightier than we."
>
> So they appointed taskmasters over them to afflict them with hard labor. And they built for Pharaoh Storage cities, Pithom and Raamses…
>
> The Egyptians compelled the sons of Israel to

Larry A. Brown Sr.

labor rigorously; and they made their lives bitter
with hard labor in mortar and bricks and at all
kinds of labor in the field, all their labors which they
rigorously imposed on them.

Exodus 1:7–9, 11, 13–14

"They put them into slavery. Why did you let this
happen?"

For through the grace given to me I say to everyone
among you not to think *more highly of himself* than
he ought to think; but to think so as to have sound
judgment, as God has allotted to each a measure of
faith.

Romans 12:3

They have quickly turned aside from the way which I
commanded them. *They have made a molten calf,* and
have worshipped it and have sacrificed to it and said,
"This is your god, O Israel, who brought you up
from the land of Egypt!"

Exodus 32:8

"They forgot who I was! They were following the gods of
the Egyptians. When they finally realized this, they cried
out, and I heard them."
    "They don't get it, do they?"
    "Unfortunately, few do, which saddens me greatly!"

Now it came about in the course of those many days
that the king of Egypt died. And the sons of Israel
sighed because of the bondage, and they cried out;

and their cry for help because of their bondage rose up to God. So God heard their *groaning*; and God remembered His covenant with Abraham, Isaac, and Jacob. God saw the sons of Israel, and God took notice of them.

Exodus 2:23–25

Let's Talk about Moses

Now Moses was pasturing the flock of Jethro his father-in-law, the priest of Midian; and he led the flock to the west side of the wilderness and came to Horeb, the mountain of God.

Exodus 3:1

"Is this the same Moses that was put in the basket and placed into the river?"

"Yes, the same."

Now a man from the house of Levi went and married a daughter of Levi. The woman conceived and bore a son; and when she saw that he was beautiful, she hid him for three months.

Exodus 2:1–2

"Why would she hide him?"

Then the Pharaoh commanded all his people, saying, "Every son who is born you are to cast into the Nile, and every daughter you are to keep alive."

Exodus 1:22

Larry A. Brown Sr.

"So Egypt feared the growth of Israel and tried to control them, right?"

"Right."

> The daughter of Pharaoh came down to bathe at the Nile, with her maidens walking alongside the Nile; and she saw the basket among the reeds and sent her maid, and she brought it to her.
>
> The child grew, and she brought him to Pharaoh's daughter and he became her son. And she named him Moses, and said, "Because I drew him out of the water."
>
> Exodus 2:5, 10

> Moses was learned in all the wisdom of the Egyptians, and was mighty in words and in deeds.
>
> Acts 7:22 (KJV)

"So what you are saying is that you protected Moses from being killed by the Egyptians so he could deliver your people out of Egypt just like you did with Joseph?"

"Now you're seeing the big picture, and it's starting to develop in your mind that I am in full control! Always! It is always about the blood!"

> But when he [Moses] was approaching the age of forty, it entered his mind…
>
> Acts 7:23

"That was from you, right?"

"Right! You're learning!"

> …to visit his brethren, the sons of Israel. And when he saw one of them being treated unjustly, he defended him and took vengeance for the oppressed by striking down the Egyptian. And he supposed that his brethren understood that GOD was granting them deliverance through him, but they did not understand.
>
> Acts 7:23–25

"Wow! These people were something, weren't they?"
"Yes, they were; this is why I established the law!"

> However, you are not in the flesh but in the Spirit, if indeed the *Spirit of God dwells in you.* But if anyone does not have the *Spirit of Christ*, he does not belong to Him [Christ].
>
> Romans 8:9

"This is very important to understand, so listen!"

> Therefore, my brethren, you also *were made to die to the law through the body of Christ*, so that you might be joined to another [Christ], to Him who was raised from the dead, in order that we might bear fruit for God. For while we were in the flesh, the sinful passions, which were aroused by the law, were at work in the members of our body to bear fruit for death. But now we have been released from the law, having died to that by which we were bound, so that we serve in newness of the Spirit and not in oldness of the letter. What shall we say then? Is the law sin? May it never be! On the contrary, *I would not have come to know sin except through the law; for I would not*

Larry A. Brown Sr.

have known about coveting if *the law* had not said, "*You shall not covet.*" But sin, taking opportunity through the commandment, produced in me coveting of every kind; for *apart from the law, sin is dead.* I was once alive apart from the law; but when the commandments came, sin became alive and I died.

Romans 7:4–9

"Take a close look at this statement; it is very important to understand."

Therefore, just as through one man *sin entered into the world,* and *death through sin,* and so death spread to all men, because all sinned for until the law, sin was in the world, but sin is not imputed [counted] when there is no law. Nevertheless death reigned from *Adam until Moses,* even over those who had not sinned in the likeness of the offense of Adam, who is a type of Him who was to come.

Romans 5:12–14

"So what you are saying is that the sin committed between the lives of Adam and Moses didn't count. You chose those who you wanted and blessed them when they honored you as their God and punished them when they didn't, right?"

"Right."

"Then why did the law come in?"

The law came in so that the transgression would increase; but where sin increased, grace abounded all the more, so that as sin reigned in death, even so grace would reign through righteousness to eternal life through Jesus Christ our Lord.

Romans 5:20–21

"You made everyone accountable for his or her actions Right?"

"Right! Let me show you the reason."

Then the Lord spoke to Moses, "Depart, go up from here, you and the people whom you have brought up from the land of Egypt, to the land of which I swore to Abraham, Isaac, and Jacob, saying, 'To your descendants I will give it.' "I will send an angel before you and I will drive out the Canaanite, the Amorite, the Hittite, the Perizzite, the Hivite, and the Jebusite. "Go up to a land flowing with milk and honey; for I will not go up in your midst, because you are an obstinate [stiff-necked] people, and I might destroy you on the way."

Exodus 33:1–3

"You allowed the law to come into the world, allowing sin to abound. Because you were preparing for your Son to come and take it upon himself at the cross by the shedding of his blood, our sins gone forever. This is what you did with Joseph and Moses, sending them ahead to prepare the way for your chosen people. So the law was enacted to prepare a path for the grafting of the Gentiles into your chosen people, right?"

"The Holy Spirit has revealed this to you!"

I say then they [the Jews] did not stumble so as to fall, did they? May it never be! But by their transgression salvation has come to the Gentiles, to make them [the Jews] jealous.

Romans 11:11

"You're always in control?"
"Always!"

Do not think I came to abolish *the law or the Prophets*; I did not come to abolish but to fulfill. For truly I say to you, until heaven and earth pass away, *not the smallest letter or stroke shall pass away from the law until all is accomplished.*

Matthew 5:17–18

In everything, therefore, treat people the same way you want them to treat you, for *this is the law and the Prophets.*

Matthew 7:12

Remember that you were at that time separate from Christ, excluded from the commonwealth of Israel, strangers to the covenants of promise having no hope and without God in the world. But now in Christ Jesus you who formerly were far off have been brought near by the *blood* of Christ.

Ephesians 2:12–13

"I get it now! It's all about the blood!"
"Yes, it is!"

> For He Himself is our peace, who made both groups into one and broke down the barrier of the dividing wall, by abolishing in His Flesh *the enmity, which is the law* of commandments contained in ordinances, so that in Himself He might make the two into one new man, thus establishing peace and might reconcile them both in one body to GOD through the *cross*, by it having put to death the enmity ... for through Him we both have our access in one Spirit to the Father.
>
> Ephesians 2:14–16, 18

"Lord, why did you say that you *will not* abolish the law in Matthew 5:17 and then say in Ephesians 2:15 that *you abolished* it?"

"The text was written for two different groups of people. Notice the end of Matthew 5:18. What does it say?"

"It says, 'not the smallest letter or stroke shall pass away from the law until all is accomplished.'"

"All this is not accomplished until my chosen people accept my Son. That will happen upon his return in the last days. For every knee will bow, every tongue confess ... my Son is Lord."

"Then it is accomplished!"

> So that He may establish your hearts without blame in holiness before our God and Father at the coming of our Lord Jesus with all His saints.
>
> 1 Thessalonians 3:13

"For the people who accept my Son, the law is abolished by his blood!"

Larry A. Brown Sr.

> Seeing it is one God which shall justify the circumcised [Jewish] *by* faith and uncircumcised [Gentile] *through* faith.
>
> Romans 3:30 (KJV)

"So the law is alive and dead at the same time?"

"You are right."

> For I do not want you, brethren, to be uninformed of this mystery—so that you will not be wise in your own estimation—that a partial hardening has happened to Israel, until the fullness of the Gentiles has come in.
>
> Romans 11:25

> Therefore, my brethren, you also were made to die to the law through the body of Christ, so that you might be joined to another, to Him who was raised from the dead, in order that we might bear fruit for GOD.
>
> Romans 7:4

"Let them who have ears hear!"

"Now that we understand the law and that it is the guiding light to sin, what happens now? You abolished the law, but the law was put in place for your people to be held accountable for their actions so they could be cleansed and saved. So if you abolished the law, then you have abolished the rules that were in the law; without the rules in places for us to follow, we cannot break them causing us to sin. Right?"

"Right!"

"Wow! What did that mean?"

"It means you are correct when you stated that without the law there is no sin."

"How can that be? There is sin, isn't there?"

> Therefore by the deeds of the law there shall no flesh be justified in His sight; for by the law is the knowledge of sin.
>
> Romans 3:20 (KJV)

"John the Baptist said, 'Behold the lamb of God who takes away the sins of the world.' That is how I did it."

"How?"

"I abolished the law."

> Because the law worketh wrath, for where no law is, there is no transgression.
>
> Romans 4:15 (KJV)

"Those who accept me are not under the law and its unforgiving sin. So for those *who accept* the call from the Father, there is *no unforgiving sin*."

"What about those who *do not* accept the call? What happens then?"

> He who is not with Me is against Me; and he who does not gather with Me scatters. Therefore I say to you, any sin and blasphemy shall be forgiven people, but blasphemy against the Spirit shall not be forgiven. Whoever speaks a word against the Son of Man, it shall be forgiven him; but whoever speaks

against the Holy Spirit, it will not be forgiven him, either in this age or the age to come.

Matthew 12:30–32

For if we sin willfully after that which we have received the knowledge of the truth, there remaineth no more sacrifice for sins.

Hebrews 10:26 (KJV)

"What does that mean?"

"This means that a person who is being called by the Father out of this world and refuses to accept his call continues in his sin. I have already died and taken upon myself their sins, if they would only accept my Father's call. Instead, they become the sons of disobedience."

In which you formally walked according to the course of this world, according to the prince of the power of the air, of the spirit that is now working in the sons of disobedience.

Ephesians 2:2

Let no one deceive you with empty words, for because of these things the wrath of God comes upon the sons of disobedience.

Ephesians 5:6

For it is because of these things that the wrath of God will come upon the sons of disobedience.

Colossians 3:6

> For the wrath of God is revealed from heaven against
> all ungodliness and unrighteousness of men who
> suppress the truth in unrighteousness.
>
> Romans 1:18

"Are you saying that the wrath of God is coming because of the disobedience of the one who is called?"

"No. What I am saying is that they have a choice and the ones who make the decision not to accept my call. My wrath will be upon them just as the others."

"What do you mean by the others?"

"Remember the people before the flood, the sons of man?"

"Yes."

"The same thing happened after the flood. These are the others."

> And the field is the world; and as for good seed,
> these are the sons of the kingdom; and the bad tares
> are the sons of the evil one.
>
> Matthew 13:38

"I am not only destroying the ungodly; I am also cleansing the earth from the diseases that man brought upon himself."

"Wow! You're in control, aren't you?"

"Yes, I am! It is very humorous to me that this world thinks it knows what is good for my earth. Instead of looking to the Creator for how it all works and studying the Bible for the answers, they feel the answers are within their created brain, already knowing what is good for *my* creation!

"This world thinks my creation needs their control,

and they are going to enact the necessary changes to protect my creation! The real reason they are doing this is because of the finality of the end, as stated in my word. They are looking for the answers to stop this from happening. Satan knows the end is near! Did you know…?"

- …That the amount of toxic chemicals released into the atmosphere from vehicles since the beginning of the automobile will not add up to the amount of toxic chemicals released from just one volcanic eruption?
- …The entire population of the world since the beginning of time, if placed side-by-side front to back, wouldn't even fill up the state of Vermont?
- …That the amount of food subsidized by the industrial leaders in this world could feed the entire world's population ten times over?
- …That 2.6 people die every minute in this world; that means 82 million a year.

"The choice they made is where they are! There is nothing wrong with my created world. It is the people that have caused the problems."

This means that…

- The ozone layer is fine.
- The land verse population growth is fine.
- The food supply in this world is fine.
- Eighty-two million people a year are making their choices of where they are going.
- The reality is, the greed of the people in this world is horrendous.

"The chemical and environmental warfare that man has created in this world is a problem. The pride and greed of these people are causing an unbalance in the way the earth reproduces itself. They want more and bigger products so they create ways to fake out the system. Its people want to destroy other people, so they come up with manmade chemicals and release these chemicals into the environment. Victory they say! I say stupid!

"This alone is creating an immune system within the microorganism's world that will cause more diseases than they can even imagine! The immune systems of these microorganisms are adjusting to the increased chemicals infusing into the earth."

"These brilliant people are killing themselves from within; all for money and power?"

"It is my Earth, and my Earth is just fine!"

"The people are nuts!"

This world has tried to destroy my children from the beginning of time with no success. They think that eliminating my children and the countries that support them will bring peace to the earth and victory for their gods. This is what this world absolutely does not understand: I am in control and I will intervene! How my children respond will control the world's outcome. It has nothing to do with what the world does or its gods.

"I have been calling my children to me since the beginning of time. Now that it is coming to the end, the world has to make a choice to either accept my Son as their Savior (and I will protect them with eternal life) or to not choose my Son as their Savior (and I will destroy them)."

Much more then, having now been justified by His blood, we shall be saved from the wrath of God through Him.

Romans 5:9

Section 12: The Kingdoms

"As I was reading the book of Matthew, I came across this verse. Can you explain this to me?"

"This is very important to understand, so listen! Those who have ears let them hear!"

> And Jesus said to His disciples, "Truly I say to you, it is hard for a rich man to enter the kingdom of heaven. Again I say to you, it is easier for a camel to go through the eye of a needle, than for a rich man to enter the kingdom of GOD."
>
> Matthew 19:23–24

"They are two different places yet both the same, just as the law. Let me explain."

> When the disciples heard it, they were exceedingly amazed saying, "Who then can be saved?"
>
> Matthew 19:25 (KJV)

"They did not realize that the kingdom was right in front of them."

> Strengthening the souls of the disciples, encouraging them to continue in the faith, and saying, "Through many tribulations *we must enter the kingdom of* GOD."
>
> Acts 14:22

"They were speaking to people that were already saved when they said this. So the kingdom of God is somewhere else."

"Now you're starting to understand."

> Do not worry then, saying, "What will we eat?" or "What will we drink?" or "What will we wear for clothing?" For the Gentiles eagerly seek all these things; for your heavenly Father knows that you need these things. *But* seek first His kingdom and His righteousness *and all these things will be added to you.*
>
> Matthew 6:31–33

"Again, he is talking to saved people. You cannot seek his kingdom when you are already in it and saved, unless it is in a different place, right?"

"Right! Now, go back to Romans 8:9. Notice the three understandings of the Spirit: I am, he is, and you are.

- I am God
- He is my Son
- You are my chosen

> When you accept my Son, my Spirit comes into you, and you become *saved*.
>
> Romans 8:9

From Him

> When you start communicating with my Son, you have a *relationship*.
>
> Romans 8:10

Through Him

> When your relationship with My Son grows, *we* will come and abide in you and you become *God's will*.
>
> Romans 8:11, John 14:23

To Him

> For from Him and through Him and to Him are all things. To Him be the glory forever. Amen.
>
> Romans 11:36

"You had asked me a question pertaining to this in the beginning. Do you remember what it was?"

"Yes, I remember. I asked, 'Lord, how do I get through these steps?' This was when you didn't respond right away, and I thought you left me and our book was done."

"I didn't leave you; it was just not the time. We had to go through all these sections to understand this very important part. This is very important to understand, so listen! Those who have ears let them hear!"

> Jesus answered them, "Destroy this temple and in three days I will raise it up." The Jews then said, "It took forty-six years to build this temple, and You will raise it up in three days?" But He was speaking of the *temple* of His body.
>
> John 2:19–21

> For through Him we both have our access in one Spirit to the Father. So then you are no longer strangers and aliens, but you are fellow citizens with the saints, and are of God's household, having been built on the foundation of the apostles and prophets, Christ Jesus Himself being the corner stone, in whom the whole building, being fitted together, is growing into a *holy temple* in the Lord.
>
> Ephesians 2:18–21

"Listen to this!"

> In whom ye also are builded together for a habitation of God through the Spirit.
>
> Ephesians 2:22 (KJV)

Larry A. Brown Sr.

"The kingdom of God is for my children who have accepted my Son, receiving his salvation grace. The kingdom of heaven is for my children who were chosen by the Father in the Old Testament. They both lead to the Father's will."

> For we maintain that a man is justified by faith apart from the works of the law. Or is God the God of the Jews only? Is He the God of the Gentiles also? Yes, of Gentiles also, since indeed God who will justify the circumcised *by* faith [Jews] and the uncircumcised *through* faith [Gentiles] is one.
>
> Romans 3:28–30

1. Under the law: The way to my Father was through works.
2. Salvation grace: The way to my Father is through me.

> Jesus said unto him, I am the way, the truth, and the life. No one cometh to the Father but by Me.
>
> John 14:6 (KJV)

- The law used the physical building of the temple: the outer court, the women's court, the inner court, and the Holy Of Holies.
- The salvation grace of God uses my Son as its temple; he also has: the outer court, the women's court, the inner court, and the Holy of Holies.

"Receive the saving grace of God. (The entrance to the outer court.) This is a free gift from the Father. By accepting my son, I will send my Holy Spirit into your heart. Let's follow this together."

Salvation

That if you confess with your mouth Jesus is Lord, and believe in your heart that God raised him from the dead you will be saved; for *with the heart* a person believes, resulting in righteousness and *with the mouth* he confesses resulting in salvation.

Romans 10:9–10

Who so ever denieth the Son the same hath not the Father; he that acknowledgeth the Son hath the Father also.

1 John 2:23 (KJV)

But the Helper, the Holy Spirit, whom the father will send in My name, He will teach you all things, and bring to your remembrance all that I said to you.

John 14:26

Now we have received not the spirit of this world, but the Spirit who is from God, so that we may know the things freely given to us from God.

1 Corinthians 2:12

But now having been freed from sin and enslaved to God, you derive your benefit, resulting in sanctification, and the outcome, eternal life. For the wages of sin is death, but the *free gift* of God is eternal life in Christ Jesus our Lord.

Romans 6:22–23

"Now that you have received my Holy Spirit, this has *saved you*. Let's start working on your heart to righteousness."

Jesus

That if you confess with your mouth Jesus is Lord, and believe in your heart that God raised Him from the dead you will be saved; for with the heart a person believes, resulting in righteousness, and with the mouth he confesses resulting in salvation.

Romans 10:9–10

Abide in Me, and I in you. As the branch cannot bear fruit of itself unless it abides in the vine, so neither can you unless you abide in Me. I am the vine you are the branches; he who abides in Me and I in him, he bears much fruit, for apart from Me *you can do nothing*.

John 15:4–5

For who has known the mind of the Lord, that He may instruct him? *But we have the mind of Christ.*

1 Corinthian 2:16 (KJV)

Do not be conformed to this world, but be transformed by the renewing of your mind, so that you may prove what the will of God is, that which is good and acceptable and perfect.

Romans 12:2

Therefore prepare your minds for action, keep sober in spirit, fix your hope completely on the grace to be brought to you at the revelation of Jesus Christ.

1 Peter 1:13

And He [Jesus] who searches the hearts knows what the mind of the Spirit is, because He intercedes for the saints [us] according to the will of God.

Romans 8:27

We know that no one who is born of God sins; *but He who was born of God keeps him, and the evil one does not touch* him. We know that we are of God, and that the whole world lies in the power of the evil one. And we know that the Son of God has come, and has given us understanding so that we may know Him who is true; and *we are in Him* who is true, *in His Son Jesus Christ.* This is the true God and eternal life.

1 John 5:18–20

God

We have come to know and have *believed the love* which God has for us. *God is love,* and the one who abides in love abides in God, and *God abides in him.*

1 John 4:16

For Christ also hath once suffered for sins, the just for the unjust, so that He might *bring us to God,* having been put to death in the flesh, *but made alive by the Spirit.*

1 Peter 3:18

Jesus answered and said to him, "If anyone *loves Me,* he will keep My word; and My Father will love him, and *we* will come to him and make Our abode with him.

John 14:23

Larry A. Brown Sr.

For in Christ Jesus neither circumcision nor uncircumcision means anything, but faith working through Love.

Galatians 5:6

Blessed be the GOD and Father of our Lord Jesus Christ, who has blessed us with every spiritual blessing in the heavenly places *in Christ,* just as HE chose us in Him before the foundation of the world, that we would be holy and blameless before *Him in Love.*

Ephesians 1:3–4

"Please understand this without any bias or judgment. I love you personally just as you are right now! Come to me who are worried, and I will give you rest."

1. Accept Jesus as Lord and Savior!

   Outer Court

   _____

   Receiving the Holy Spirit in your heart

2. Having a relationship with Jesus!
   Receiving Jesus' Spirit in you
   "Fruits of the Holy Spirit"

3. Walking and growing in Jesus by studying the Word with him, allowing him to teach what the Holy Spirit is saying, and guiding you to the Father's will!

4. Understanding that God loves you!

Receiving God's Spirit in you
Inner court: walking with God

Now the triune Spirit has made their home in you, the Holy Spirit, Jesus' Spirit, and the Father's Spirit.

"Power of the Holy Spirit!"

"You are now walking and growing in God, understanding his will, and utilizing his powers."

> That if you confess with your mouth Jesus as Lord and believe in your heart that GOD raised him from the dead, you will be saved; for with the heart a person believes, resulting in righteousness, and with the mouth he confesses, resulting in salvation.
>
> Romans 10:9–10

> However you are not in the flesh but in the Spirit, if indeed the Spirit of GOD dwells in you. {Holy Spirit}
>
> Romans 8:9

> If Christ is in you, though the body is dead because of sin, yet the spirit is alive because of righteousness. {Christ's Spirit}
>
> Romans 8:10

> But if the *Spirit of Him who raised Jesus from the dead* dwells in you, He who raised Christ Jesus from the dead will also give life to your mortal bodies through His Spirit who dwells in you. {God's Spirit}
>
> Romans 8:11

Jesus answered and said to him, "If anyone loves

Me, he will keep My word; and My Father will love him and WE *will come to him and make Our abodes [residence] with him.*

John 14:23

I am the way, the truth and the life: No man cometh unto the Father, but by me.

John 14:6 (KJV)

The Temple of Christ

"This is the way it works. You must adhere to the calling of my Father to bring you out of the world. The only way to do this is by accepting me (Jesus Christ), as your personal savior. If you do not adhere to the call of the Father, then you commit blasphemy of the Holy Spirit! For what does it profit a man if he gains the whole world and forfeits his soul?

"I already died for your sins, and if you do not accept that, then there is nothing to talk about with me anymore, is there? For by your words you will be justified, and by your words you will be condemned! Here are the steps to enter into the temple."

Entrance into the outer court of Jesus!

"Accepting his call; my Father sends his Holy Spirit into your heart, assuring your entrance into heaven. Now you are in this state of existence until you die. You will enter with nothing but the 'free ticket' that comes with confessing me as Lord. In heaven—where the free ticket people go—that is where you will be!

"Do not store up for yourself treasures on earth, where

the moths and the rust destroy and where thieves break in and steal it, but store up for you treasures in heaven. By receiving the free gift of the Holy Spirit, this entitles you to a relationship with me."

"The Holy Spirit enters you as a mustard seed, planted by my Father to grow you into a mature person for his will. Some people call this 'born again.' But this is my Father's saving grace, freely given to all who accept his call. This is not what I meant by 'born again.' This is *the beginning of the birthing process in me.*

"As you move into this relationship with me, you will start receiving the knowledge that only the Word of God can bring you. This knowledge will lead you to the fruits of the Holy Spirit. Therefore as you have received Christ Jesus the Lord, so walk in him, having been firmly rooted and now being built up in him and established in your faith, just like you have been instructed.

"For in him all fullness of the deity dwells in bodily form. And in him you have been made complete, and he is the head over all rule and authority. Our relationship is the only way of understanding my Father's will. No one comes to the Father unless they go through the Son. There is no condemnation for those who are in Christ."

"As you move and grow in our relationship, you start receiving the fruits of the Holy Spirit. But be careful here! I know your deeds, that you are neither cold nor hot. I wish that you were cold or hot, But because you are lukewarm; neither cold nor hot, I will spit you out of my mouth.

By becoming lukewarm in our relationship, you will

Larry A. Brown Sr.

have to repent and start the process over again. This is where my chosen people stop growing and are removed back to the beginning.

"The religious society says they are not saved. They feel that heaven *is the kingdom of God,* and if I spit you out you lose your salvation. That is not so! The kingdom of God is in the final steps in your growth in me, leading you to the power of the Holy Spirit and my Father's will for you!"

> For the kingdom of God is not in word, *but in power.*
> 1 Corinthians 4:20 (KJV)

"When you accept me as your Savior; My Father's saving grace enters you as a free gift and cannot be won or lost! It is received at your conversion."

> And Jesus said to his disciples, "Truly I say to you, it is hard for a rich man *to enter the kingdom of heaven*; again I say to you, it is easier for a camel to go through the eye of a needle, than a *rich man to enter into the kingdom of* GOD" *(Matthew 19:23–24).*

Entrance into the inner court (kingdom of God) with Jesus!
"Unless you are born again, *you cannot see* the *kingdom of God.* Truly I say to you, whoever does not receive the kingdom of God like a child will not enter it. Permit the children to come to me and do not hinder them, *for the kingdom of God belongs to such as these.* Now the deeds of the flesh are evident:

- Immorality
- Impurity
- Sensuality
- Idolatry
- Sorcery
- Enmities
- Strife
- Jealousy
- Outburst of anger
- Disputes
- Dissensions
- Factions
- Envying
- Drunkenness
- Carousing

" … and things like these, of which I forewarn you, just as I have forewarned you, that those who practice such things would not inherit the kingdom of God. Some people will tell you that if you struggle with any of these things, then you cannot be saved. That is wrong!"

> Come to Me all who are worried and I will give you rest. Take My yoke and learn from Me, for I am of gentleness and you will find rest for your souls; for My yoke is easy and light.
>
> Matthew 11:28–30

"When you accept *my* Son as your personal Savior, *you are in all of these practices.* In a relationship with my Son, these

Larry A. Brown Sr.

worldly practices can and will be turned into the fruit of the Spirit as you grow in this relationship."

The Fruits of the Spirit:

- Love
- Joy
- Peace
- Patience
- Kindness
- Goodness
- Faithfulness
- Gentleness
- Self-control

"In a relationship with my Son, you will grow to the point of 'graduation.' This graduation, or *born again status*, will allow you to *enter into the inner court* (Kingdom of God). Now I can use you in the purpose I created you for."

> Truly, truly I say to you, unless one is born again he cannot see the kingdom of God.
> Truly, truly I say to you unless one is born of water and the Spirit he cannot enter into the kingdom of God. That which is born of the flesh is flesh, and that which is born of the Spirit is spirit.
>
> John 3:3, 5–6

> Strengthening the souls of the disciples, encouraging them *to continue in the faith*, and saying, "Through many tribulations *we must enter* the kingdom of God." (Inner court)
>
> Acts 14:22

The Power of the Holy Spirit:

- Word of Wisdom
- Word of Knowledge
- Faith
- Gift of Healing
- Effecting of Miracles
- Prophecy
- Distinguishing of Spirits
- Various kinds of Tongues
- Interpretation of Tongues

> Blessed is a man who perseveres under trial, *for once he has been approved,* he will receive the crown [badge of royalty] of life [living life abundantly] which the Lord has promised to those who love Him.
>
> James 1:12

"Thank you for the help with the scriptures."
"You're welcome."

Larry A. Brown Sr.

Section 13: Born Again

So Jesus said to them, "Truly, truly, I say to you, *unless you eat the flesh of the Son of Man* and *drink His blood*, you have no life in yourselves. *He who eats My flesh* and *drinks My blood has eternal life*, and I will raise him up on the last day. For My flesh is true food, and My blood is true drink.

John 6:53–54

"Wow! What does that mean?"
    "This is very important, so follow closely!"

> He that eateth My flesh and drinketh My blood
> *dwelleth in Me, and I in him.*
>
> John 6:56 (KJV)

When you accept my Son, my Spirit comes and lives in your heart, and you are saved, right?"

"Right!"

> But the helper, the Holy Spirit, whom the Father will
> send in My name, He will teach you all things, and
> bring to your remembrance all that I have said to you.
>
> John 14:26

> I [Jesus] will ask the Father and *He will give you another*
> *Helper,* that He may be with you forever; that is *the*
> *Spirit of truth,* whom the world cannot receive, because
> it does not see Him or know Him, but you know Him
> because *He abides with you and will be in you.*
>
> John 14:16–17

> However, you are not in the flesh but in the Spirit, if
> indeed the Spirit of God dwells in you.
>
> Romans 8:9

> He came to his own, and those who were His own
> did not receive Him. But as *many as received Him,* to
> them *He gave the right to become the children of God,*
> *even to those who believe in His name.*
>
> John 1:11–12

"Please follow this closely!

"Now that you are saved, you have a choice to make: to

have a relationship with my Son or not. If you choose this relationship, you will enter into my Son's Spirit. At the very beginning of the relationship with my son, you are as a child in a mother's womb. The child is solely dependent on the nutrients that come from the mother's blood to sustain its life while growing into an independent, living being. I created this from the beginning with Eve, right?"

"Right!"

"This is what my Son was talking about when he was stating that you must eat *his flesh* and *drink his blood.*"

> But as many as received Him, to them He gave the right to become children of God, even to those who believe in His Name, *who were born* not of blood nor of the will of the flesh nor of the will of man, *but of God.*
>
> John 1:12–13

"When you have a relationship with my Son, you abide in his spiritual womb just like an unborn child does. This spiritual womb gives you the nutrients that the word (the Bible) has to offer, while being sustained by his blood."

> It is the spirit who gives life; the flesh profits nothing; the words that I have spoken to you are spirit and are life.
>
> John 6:63

"Please listen! This spiritual growth within the womb of my Son grooms you for my will. This also prepares you for when I will come and abide in you."

Jesus answered and said to him, "If anyone loves Me, he will keep My Word; and My Father will love him, and *we will come to him and make our abode [home] with him.*

John 14:23

But if the Spirit of Him who *raised Jesus from the dead dwells in you,* He who raised Christ Jesus from the dead will also *give life to your mortal bodies through His Spirit* who dwells in you.

Romans 8:11

"Now I can and will use you by distributing the *power of the Holy Spirit* as I see fit."

"People think that you are 'born again' at the salvation grace of acceptance. The *salvation grace of my Father* is when his Holy Spirit comes into your life and then you are saved."

Your relationship with *my* Son grooms you and prepares you for Our Spirits to make our homes in you.

John 14:23

"You will be birthed out of this relationship and into the power of the Holy Spirit."

But if the Spirit of Him who raised Jesus from the dead dwells in you, *He who raised Christ Jesus from the dead* will also *give life to your mortal bodies through His Spirit who dwells in you.*

Romans 8:11

"You are then born again!"

His resurrection has all the answers!

Larry A. Brown Sr.

Section 14: The God Walking Oath

And since we have a great priest over the house of God, let us draw near with a sincere heart in full assurance of faith, having our hearts sprinkled clean from the evil conscience and our bodies washed with pure water. Let us hold fast the confession of our hope without wavering, for He who promised is faithful; and let us consider how to stimulate one another to love and good deeds, not forsaking our own assembling together, as is the habit of some, but encouraging one another; and all the more as you see the day drawing near.

Hebrews 10:21–25

"I love you, and I demonstrated it when I died for you personally on the cross. Now I am offering to have a relationship with you. Together we will walk into the Father's will. Let me show you the mysteries of the Bible and how they're intended just for you!"

Section 15: A Relationship in Christ

That if you confess with your mouth Jesus as Lord,
and believe in your heart that GOD *raised him from the
dead,* you will be saved; for with the heart a person
believes, resulting in righteousness, and with the
mouth he confesses, resulting in salvation.

Romans 10:9–10

The Resurrection

"This is the first thing that you will learn and believe in
whole heartedly as we start to move in our relationship
together. Without this belief, our relationship will mean

nothing, and the power that comes from this understanding will not be effective. My presence and my ministry on this earth for you will be powerless. We must come together in this truth, for this is reality. This understanding is the only way we can start to move into the Father's will for you. Look at these scriptures and *believe!*"

> But GOD, being rich in mercy, because of His great love with which He Loved us, even when we were dead in our transgressions, made us alive together with Christ (by grace you have been saved), and raised us up with Him and seated us with Him in the Heavenly places in Christ Jesus.
>
> Ephesians 2:4–6

> Therefore we have been buried with Him through baptism into death, so that as Christ was raised from the dead through the glory of the Father, so we too might walk in the newness of life. For if we have become united with Him in the likeness of His death, certainly we shall also be in the likeness of His resurrection, knowing this, that our old self was crucified with Him, in order that our body of sin might be done away with, so that we would no longer be slaves to sin; for he who has died is free from sin.
>
> *Knowing that Christ*, having been raised from the dead, is never to die again; death no longer is master over Him. For the death that He died, He died to sin once for all; but the life that He lives, He lives to GOD.
>
> But now having been freed from sin and enslaved to GOD, you derive your benefit, resulting in sanctification, and the outcome, *eternal life*.
>
> For the wages of sin is death, but the free gift of

Larry A. Brown Sr.

GOD is *eternal life* in Christ Jesus our Lord.

Romans 6:4–7, 8–10, 22–23

And if Christ has not been raised, then our preaching is vain, your faith also is vain and if Christ has not been raised, your faith is worthless; and you are still in your sins

1 Corinthians 15:14, 17

"You must believe in my resurrection, and then you can truly believe in me!

"If my Father did not raise me from the dead, then I am still in the grave, and you cannot have a relationship with a dead person; but I am alive! I am here waiting for you. Believe in my resurrection, and we can walk together."

"There is so much that the Bible has to offer; if we wrote it all down, we would have to write the entire Bible, for every sentence has a meaning for each one of us."

Then Jesus said, "May I interject a thought here?"

"Okay."

"I would like to extend an invitation to the readers, asking them if they would like to study the word with me. Here are some studies we could do together:

We could talk about…

- … King David, and why I picked him over all his brothers, or why my people needed a king in the first place.
- … why Matthew's version of the bloodline from David to my Son differs from Luke's account of the same bloodline.

- … the marvels of the Psalms, who wrote them, and learning how they can be a great influence in life.

"In every study we have together, you will always come to the same conclusion: I am always in control and you can trust me. Let's walk together into my Father's will for you!"

"In our relationship with the teacher and counselor, Jesus Christ, we can always ask the how and why questions while studying his word with him. In doing so, he allows us to see an unbelievable sight: the Bible miraculously coming alive right in front of our eyes!"

"God be with you always."

Let's talk and find your way into my Father's will.

"Remember, if you accept my Son as your personal savior, your work is just beginning, for it is written that faith without works is nothing! On the other hand, faith with works is everything!"

> And thou shalt love the LORD thy God with all thine heart, and with all thy soul, and with all thy might.
>
> Deuteronomy 6:5 (KJV)

> Love your neighbor as you love yourself.
>
> Leviticus 19:18

Larry A. Brown Sr.

Final Thoughts

We wrote this book not to challenge the Bible scholars of this world or to set any stumbling blocks for anyone who is searching out the truth.

Whether or not we were clothed by animal skin in Genesis or how the earth originated are not the questions we need to be talking about. We will all find out these things when we ask him personally.

This book points to an unwavering truth: Jesus is the way, the truth, and the life, and having a personal relationship with him will guide you to the Father's will. Stepping into this relationship will be a difficult thing to do in today's world, giving up all our freedom. But when we decide to step out in faith the opposite is true! We gain our freedom in the fruit of the Spirit and the power of a living God.

"Let's talk and find out this truth."

A relationship with Jesus is needed to achieve this powerful degree in life. No money is needed; there are no long essays to write before admission, and no thesis needed for your doctorate. Just apply, and you're automatically accepted. The degree you receive is in the will of the Father! And your accolades are eternal!

The Letter

My Dearest Son,

This is my gift to you because you loved me all the way through your hurts, your doubts, your sorrows, but most of all, your understanding of me. Victory cries out! Victory cries out! For it is done! For you, my Son! My son, here is your bride, the Holy City of Jerusalem. This is how John saw it in the book of Revelation:

> I saw the holy city, the New Jerusalem, coming down out of heaven from God, prepared as a bride beautifully dressed for her husband. And I heard

a loud voice from the throne, saying, "Now the dwelling of God is with men, and He will live with them. They will be His people and God Himself will be with them and be their God. He will wipe away every tear from their eyes. There will be no more death or mourning or crying or pain, for the old order of things has passed away" (Revelation 21:2–4).

Always and forever,
Abba, Father

Larry A. Brown Sr.

LIVE

---

listen|imagine|view|experience

AUDIO BOOK DOWNLOAD INCLUDED WITH THIS BOOK!

In your hands you hold a complete digital entertainment package. Besides purchasing the paper version of this book, this book includes a free download of the audio version of this book. Simply use the code listed below when visiting our website. Once downloaded to your computer, you can listen to the book through your computer's speakers, burn it to an audio CD or save the file to your portable music device (such as Apple's popular iPod) and listen on the go!

How to get your free audio book digital download:

1. Visit www.tatepublishing.com and click on the e|LIVE logo on the home page.
2. Enter the following coupon code:
   da8c-d235-7a15-76d8-c3a3-9ac2-d878-4b18
3. Download the audio book from your e|LIVE digital locker and begin enjoying your new digital entertainment package today!